ROMANCE MONOGRAPHS, INC.
Number 18

MEXICO IN THE THEATER

ROMANCE MONOGRAPHS, INC.
Number 18

MEXICO
IN THE THEATER

BY

RODOLFO USIGLI

Translated with an introduction
BY
WILDER P. SCOTT

UNIVERSITY, MISSISSIPPI
ROMANCE MONOGRAPHS, INC.
1 9 7 6

Authorized translation

COPYRIGHT © 1976

BY

ROMANCE MONOGRAPHS, INC.

P.O. BOX 7553

UNIVERSITY, MISSISSIPPI 38677

PRINTED IN SPAIN

IMPRESO EN ESPAÑA

I. S. B. N. 84-399-4744-5

DEPÓSITO LEGAL: V. 169 - 1976

ARTES GRÁFICAS SOLER, S. A. - JÁVEA, 28 - VALENCIA (8) - 1976

Library of Congress Cataloging in Publication Data

Usigli, Rodolfo, 1905-

    Mexico in the theater.
    (Romance monographs; no. 18)
    Translation of México en el teatro.

    Bibliography: p.

    Includes indexes.

    1. Performing arts—Mexico—History. I. Title.

PN2311.U713   792'.0972   75-38748

TABLE OF CONTENTS

TRANSLATOR'S INTRODUCTION

AS THE AUTHOR of almost forty plays, several of which have become virtual classics of the Mexican and Spanish American stage, Rodolfo Usigli will hardly require a detailed introduction to students of the Latin American theater. *El gesticulador* (*The Great Pretender*, 1938), *Jano es una muchacha* (*Janus is a Girl*, 1952), *Corona de sombra* (*Crown of Shadows*, 1943), and *El niño y la niebla* (*The Boy and the Haze*, 1936), bear witness to Usigli's skill in the manipulation of both characters and dialogue. Little known, on the contrary, outside of Latin America, are the numerous contributions which Rodolfo Usigli has made to literary criticism and theatrical history. The playwright's tireless reading of plays and assiduous study of the theater throughout his life make of Usigli one of the most authoritative spokesmen in matters of the drama both in Spanish America and throughout the Western world.

Born in Mexico City in 1905, Rodolfo Usigli witnessed as a child the chaos and destruction brought about by the Mexican Revolution. His father, Alberto Usigli, was of Italian extraction, and his mother, Carlota Wainer, was of Austro-Hungarian descent. Critics have often pointed out that the playwright's European heritage has something to do, however intangibly, with the objectivity with which he views the customs and mores of his fellow countrymen. This opinion would seem to be confirmed when one considers the number of plays devoted by Usigli to an examination of the Mexican way of life (sexual standards in *Jano es una muchacha*, national character flaws in *El gesticulador*, the life of the middle and upper economic classes in *Medio tono* (*The Great Middle Class*, 1937) and *La familia cena en casa* (*The Family Dines at Home*, 1942), respectively.

By the age of ten, Usigli was giving puppet shows for his friends. In 1917, at the age of twelve, he appeared in a stage production with the troupe of Emilia R. del Castillo and Julio Taboada at the Teatro Colón in Mexico City. In 1923 he enrolled at the Escuela Popular Nocturna de Música y Declamación. A year later he began to write theatrical reviews in the magazine *El Sábado,* then called *El Martes.* Subsequently he wrote articles on drama for *Imagen* (1932-1933), *Noticias Gráficas* (1942-1943), *Hoy* (1943), and others, and he has continued to write articles sporadically for the Mexican daily newspapers *Novedades* and *Excelsior.*

Usigli became professionally associated with the theater in 1931 when he was appointed to the faculty of the Summer School of Philosophy and Letters at the National University of Mexico as a lecturer in the history and technique of the theater. He actively wrote dramatic criticism while studying an average of ten plays per day in order to improve his acquaintance with the theater. His study of foreign languages allowed him to do most of this study in English and French, and he was soon to write one of his earliest works, *4 Chemins 4,* entirely in French. Many of his subsequent plays have passages spoken in English and French which are appropriately suited to the nationalities of the respective characters. Usigli has also used his foreign language ability to do numerous translations of foreign plays, mostly for the use of the Teatro de Orientación, which was doing foreign productions in the thirties in an effort to counteract the traditional influence of Spanish nineteenth century melodramas and *costumbrista* plays.

Although Usigli would no doubt have preferred to be staging his own works in the mid-thirties, he found them rejected repeatedly because of their attacks on Mexican customs. He did gain from his other activities, however, valuable theatrical experience which would serve him well later in his career. He also made a gallant effort, with other young people, to bring about a change in the overall theatrical climate of his homeland.

Having failed in his attempts to get his first play produced, *El apóstol (The Apostle,* 1931), Usigli decided to accept a Rockefeller Foundation grant for the study of drama at Yale University during the academic year 1935-36. He roomed while there with his fellow Mexican playwright Xavier Villaurrutia. Together they studied techniques of dramatic composition and production. The time spent at Yale, which provided Usigli an opportunity for uninterrupted work, also allowed him to study the works of his favorite writers: Shaw, Behrman, Rice, Anderson, O'Neill and Odets.

Upon his return to Mexico City in 1936, Usigli continued writing poetry and drama. He was appointed head of the theatrical section of the Instituto Nacional de Bellas Artes. On November 13, 1937, his first play to be produced in Mexico City, *Medio tono,* was staged at the Palacio de Bellas Artes by the dramatic company of María Teresa Montoya. It was received badly by critics and caused a storm of critical controversy. Two years later, however, the production of *La mujer no hace milagros (Women Can't Work Miracles,* 1938), at the Teatro Ideal, caused an even greater critical embroglio.

In 1940 Usigli published an account of his stay at Yale, but his creation of the ill-fated Teatro de Medianoche was by far the most important event of that year. Intended originally to be used almost exclusively for the production of works by Mexican authors, some nine plays were produced over a period of six weeks in March and April of 1940. The theater had to be disbanded because of the vituperative attacks of conservatively oriented critics.

Discouraged by his inability to have his works produced successfully, and in part because of the confusion brought about by the beginning of World War II, Usigli entered the Mexican diplomatic corps in 1944. He was sent to Paris, where he became Second Secretary at the Mexican Embassy, a post which he held until 1946. This two year stay was to afford him the opportunity to contact personally two of the writers whom he most admired, George Bernard Shaw and Jean Anouilh.

It was on May 17, 1947, that Usigli's play *El gesticulador,* presented at the Palacio de Bellas Artes, produced a virtual storm of protest. The drama united those critics who had previously attacked his works on political and aesthetic grounds and thrust him swiftly into the role of *enfant terrible* of the Mexican stage. Only four years later, however, events were to take a sudden turn. The production of *El niño y la niebla* in 1951, a play influenced by Ibsen which dealt with a case of hereditary insanity, was acclaimed by critics and public alike. Usigli, virtually for the first time, had not levelled his by now customary dramatic attack on some aspect of Mexican life. After twenty years of writing and producing plays, he had become acceptable in Mexican theatrical circles. While subsequent productions of his plays, *Jano es una muchacha* (1952), and *Corona de fuego* (*Crown of Fire*, 1963), among others, generated some controversy, the dramatist received more and more critical acclaim and audience acceptance. By the beginning of the sixties, Rodolfo Usigli was a venerated and acknowledged major figure in the drama in Mexico and Spanish America. Television adaptations, film versions, and foreign translations and productions of his plays multiplied apace to the point where his status as a dramatist was recently described by Professor Luis Leal of the University of Illinois, in his *Breve Historia de la Literatura Hispanoamericana* (New York: Alfred Knopf, 1971) in the following terms: "Rodolfo Usigli (Mexico, 1905) is without any doubt the most representative Spanish American dramatist of this period (1940-1970)" (p. 298).

In 1957 Usigli was sent to Beirut, Lebanon, as Minister Plenipotentiary of Mexico where he remained until his assignment as Mexican Ambassador to Norway in 1960. Since retiring from the diplomatic service in Oslo in 1972, Usigli has returned to Mexico City where he is continuing, at the age of sixty-seven, to write additional plays and theatrical criticism. His efforts were rewarded in November, 1972, when he received the Premio Nacional de Letras (National Prize for Literature).

"*México en el teatro*"

The scope of Usigli's familiarity with the theater is apparent when one considers *México en el teatro* (*Mexico in the Theater*, 1932). Although this historico-critical work figures among the earliest publications by the Mexican dramatist, it is a fine example of the efforts made by Usigli to train himself academically as a playwright. It should also be mentioned that, after Enrique Olavarría y Ferrari's *Reseña Histórica del teatro en México, México en el teatro* is one of the earliest attempts by any author to study the Mexican theater as an artistic entity from pre-Columbian times to the first third of the twentieth century. Those familiar with both of these works will probably also agree that while the former work contains formidable quantities of information, the most recent edition published in Mexico consists of five volumes and a one volume index, it is less readable and concise than Usigli's work. *México en el teatro,* therefore, is profitable reading for the person who desires an overview of the trajectory of the Mexican theater from its origins to the recent past. The informal and personal style used by Usigli in *México en el teatro,* while occasionally leaving something to be desired regarding scholarly documentation (footnotes and bibliographical entries are occasionally incomplete), leaves no doubt about the book's *raison d'être*: it is a history of drama written by a playwright who does not spend time on pedantic details because he is interested in the *spirit* of Mexican theatrical history, something which cannot *per se* be subjected to ordinary historical or scholarly methodology.

It is interesting to note that Usigli, perhaps without knowing it, used the same literary technique in writing *México en el teatro* which he employed many years later in the so-called "anti-historical" trilogy of plays concerning Mexico's national, spiritual and historical development, respectively *Corona de fuego* (*Crown of Fire,* 1960), *Corona de luz* (*Crown of Light,* 1963), and *Corona de sombra* (*Crown of Shadows,* 1943). Disregarding the actual facts and sequences of events involved, the dramatist reassembled in these plays a chain of events which, while not strictly following historical accounts, better presented in a more original way the historical and artistic signific-ance of the occurrances. Essentially this same technique, in embry-onic form, is observable in *México en el teatro.* Usigli has not discussed specific works by certain Mexican dramatists in detail, nor has he attempted to mention all authors and works. He has chosen good and bad examples of both works and authors in order to arrive at a representative sample of the quality of the Mexican drama. More than anything else he has tried to trace the development of the theater in his native country in order to judge its position in the world theater. He is not content to praise it lavishly or condemn it roundly, but attempts to point out from an artistic point of view, not necessarily always an objective one, what he believes the state of the Mexican drama to be.

México en el teatro is basically structured chronologically. The author begins with the pre-Columbian theater, passes through the period of the Conquest and subsequent centuries, and reaches the beginnings of the motion picture in Mexico in the nineteen twen-ties and thirties. It is significant that his discussion of the motion picture, particularly in the essays contained in the *Appendix,* is as pithy and valid today as ever. The fundamental questions regarding the limitations and advantages of the cinematographer's art which Usigli poses have never been satisfactorily answered. One senses, however, throughout his discussions of the differences between the theater and the motion picture, that he is unalterably opposed to any art form or nascent genre which may in any way have a deleterious effect on his beloved theater, which according to him is "animated sculpture."

The evaluations which the author makes of certain outstanding Mexican dramatists and their works, for example those concerning Sor Juana Inés de la Cruz and Juan Ruiz de Alarcón, essentially involve the feelings of one artist for another. Usigli considers the artistic viewpoint manifested by any playwright to be at least as important as any one of his individual works. He sees the work of art as an expression of the mind and soul of its creator, and utilizes the characteristics of the former in order to arrive at an appreciation of both the writer's theory of art as well as his importance as a reflection of the spirit of his times.

The work has been presented here with the original format in which it appeared in 1932. The footnotes at the end of the text have been cited as Usigli formulated them with the titles of the works from which quotations are drawn left in the original Spanish. Throughout the text itself the titles of plays have been translated into English for the benefit of the reader who is unfamiliar with Spanish. The original Spanish titles of Mexican works mentioned, together with the standardized English titles used here, may be found in the third edition of Carlos González Peña's *History of Mexican Literature,* translated by Gusta Barfield Nance and Florene J. Dunstan, published by Southern Methodist University Press, Dallas, Texas, 1968. In order to maintain consistency, the names of actual theaters in Mexico City have been left in Spanish because they can be readily recognized by the English speaking reader. Certain terms referring to songs, dances and dramatic genres peculiar to Spanish or Spanish-American culture, such as *sones, danzas, zarzuelas* or *entremeses,* have been retained in the text in Spanish as they are usually familiar to those conversant to any degree with the terminology of the theater. Contextual usage, at any rate, normally makes the meaning of these words clear even when no satisfactory translation for them exists in English. The bibliography at the end of the work has been rendered into English where possible, but titles of works in Spanish have been left in their original form so that the interested reader who wishes to pursue further research would not receive the impression that they were written in English.

I would like to take this opportunity to express my sincerest appreciation to Rodolfo Usigli for the cooperation which he afforded me in granting permission to translate *México en el teatro*. His advice and counsel over the years concerning the genesis and elaboration of his dramatic theory and practices have been invaluable. His enthusiasm for the Mexican theater and his interest in its development are unequalled.

WILDER P. SCOTT

ATHENS, GEORGIA
December 15, 1972

RODOLFO USIGLI

MEXICO
IN THE THEATER

MEXICO CITY, MEXICO

MCMXXXII

To Maestro Antonio Caso,
whose words inspired this book

PANORAMA

I WILL avoid making too profound an incursion into the complicated edifices of the multiple Dedaluses of the history of the theater. In the first place because it is more dangerous to go astray knowingly than in ignorance, and next out of deference to brevity, the only truly unique thing in the world.

A timid glance at the Greek tragedians and playwrights is sufficient, however, to perceive the differences of purpose and of practice which arise between their theater and that of the Middle Ages. The tragedy, from Aeschylus to Euripides, the satirical drama, invented perhaps by Pratinas of Phlius and cultivated by Euripides in *The Cyclops,* and the comedy, from Susarion and Aristophanes to Menander and Diphilius, attest to two purposes in the Greek theater: art and criticism. This is particularly true of the comedy. The ancient comedy, with chorus, in the hands of Epicharmus and Deinolocos, of Susarion and Crates, of Cratinus, Eupolis and Aristophanes, is concerned with violence and propriety, fantasy and obscenity, the arts and customs, and politics. The lyric element of the chorus having been suppressed in the middle period, mythological themes are alternated in it with the portraits — or better yet the statues — of contemporary customs. The new comedy employs the prologue of the tragedy, and acquires types completely characteristic of those of Menander, Diphilius and Apollodorus of Carystus. In it the lady of the court and the parasite are well defined characters, expressions of racial perfection and of decadence primarily. In whatever form, the Greek theater is from one extreme of its perfect life to the other a popular artistic spectacle on the one hand, a literary one on the other.

Although under the influence of the heritage from Greece, and fascinated by the mortal games between men and beasts which were more popular, Rome offers another cycle in which, due to the proverbial paradox, the theater does not progress a great deal but does not regress very much either. If it is clothed at the beginning in the Attic *pallium* imposed upon it by Plautus, Caecilius and Terence, it bears proudly at the end the Roman symbol, and the customs and pleasures of Rome color the *commedia togata* of Lucius Afranius. Subsequently, the *atellanae* and the buffoons control the domain of public taste and the curtain falls on the declining Roman development.

With different problems, the occidental and powerful Middle Ages comprehend the diffusing force of the theater and utilize it, turning it away from its true character. The theater of customs, carried to a height of great satire and professional perfection in the ancient world, is banished in the Medieval period. Its existence as a system of propaganda — so effective in the presentation of ritual ceremonies for the gods and in the flagellation of customs for humans in numerous contests — is respected, nevertheless, and is applied to the evangelization of the multitudes in an implacable manner. The phrase of a Christian apostle has blessed the ears as the broadest and most secure portals for the passage of faith. Furthermore, the Catholic liturgy finds an appropriate place in theatrical representation, and the mysteries and *autos sacramentales* —intended at one time to evangelize the masses and to combat the popularity of the Italian minstrels after the eleventh century — threaten, inspire and convince the audience. Little by little after the minstrelsy, however, farces, *sotties* and morality plays are introduced as the popular needs are transformed in the aforementioned spiral of evolution, and they eventually become indispensable.

At this point the Renaissance — that monstruous flowering of humanity in the world — places on the Western theater a new prestige as a great art form. Ariosto, Cardinal Dovizi di Bibbiena (*La Calandria*), Cecchi, Aníbale Caro, Machiavelli, who embellishes the Italian drama with the master color of *La Mandragora,* Aretino, all develop the theater in Italy. Giovan Trissino, later, formulates the classical rules from the heights of his tragedy *Sophonisbe,* and Gelli and Dolce aid him, while the popular drama, from which the improvised play or *commedia dell' arte* will arise, is cultivated by

G. B. della Porta, Giordano Bruno and others. Spain has the *Eglogas en Acción* of Juan del Encina, and Rodrigo de Cota and Fernando de Rojas vitalize the tragedy. Later López de Villalobos, a physician and poet who attempts to succeed by means of the narrow and brilliant classical route and over whom medicine triumphs, Gil Vicente and Torres Naharro, all will broaden the theater for the translations of Simón Abril, Timoneda and the Argensolas — ancient and refined material — for Cervantes, and for the more popular work of Castillejos, Lope de Rueda and Juan de la Cueva. Jodelle and Larivey, in France, devote themselves to experiments in search of Classical formulas, particularly with their *Cléopatre,* the first example of regularity in the French tragedy. In the interspersed interludes in the performances of miracle plays from the thirteenth century onward, there arises in England the literary theatrical form which produces its pristine flower in John Heywood. Nicolas Udall represents later a definite evolution when he creates the first regular comedy of the English theater (*Ralph Roister Doister*). Udall and the hypothetical university student of Cambridge, W. Stevenson (*Gammer Gurton's Needle*) open the great roadway along which the genius of Shakespeare and the erudition of Ben Jonson will travel together, followed by Beaumont and Fletcher bearing goods from Spain. In Germany, Hans Sachs, a shoemaker from Nuremberg, establishes — the Middle Ages having past — the only theatrical frontier of the sixteenth century, which Andreas Gryphius will be the first to cross in the seventeenth century. With regard to Russia, although it has an immemorial circus, it is still in the most profound obscurity in matters pertaining to the theater. It is not until 1671 that Czar Alexis Mikhailovitch, the second of the Romanoffs, orders the first performance of religious mysteries which had been introduced into Russia by the Poles.

It is now necessary to abandon Europe on its glittering route and reject the temptation to unfold encyclopedic maps. We shall not leave, however, without pointing out that even after only a peremptory glance the European theater of the sixteenth century exhibits a more or less uniform movement in its collective protest against Medieval literature. From all the lands of the West it undertakes a return to antiquity, where the elixir of youth may be imbibed.

LANDFALL

As THE fifteenth century waned, incorrigible Jupiter descended in some form or other to the soft bed of ancient Hesperia and, in order to pay his debt, crowned her with America, a marvelous tiara if there ever was one.

In the twenty-ninth year of the Columbian era Mexico is conquered.

The period of inevitable amazement having past, the conquerors proceed to establish in the new domain the old feudal system of the division of labor: bodies and souls. Soldiers and missionaries work intensely: the former preparing the tribute for the Caesar, the latter embellishing the fabulous offering to God. The soldiers teach Spanish to the Indians; the priests learn from the Indians the secrets of the native languages. Some search only for the future, or the present; others attempt to penetrate the extraordinary past. From the soldiers and the official representatives Spain learns that there are in the conquered land undiscovered mines of gold and silver. From the priests we have a good description of the life and arts of the great neolithic races which have lost their dominions. A few, however, are fatally medieval. It is the spirit of the Middle Ages which controls and inspires in them all the deeds of construction and destruction. In order not to be absorbed or overthrown by the strength of the race they govern — powerful and complete until the Conquest — they import from Spain a duplicate of their Western life, based on the concept of a master who is hopelessly medieval, and condemn Mexico to live under the aegis of a Middle Ages more enormous and less refined than ever for as long as the Spanish dominion lasts.

We know from Fray Toribio de Benavente, from Fray Diego Durán, and from Cortés himself, that among other sciences and arts the Indians had lyric and dramatic poetry, and that they had theaters consisting of earthen platforms which were square and open and placed either in the markets or the lower atrium of some temple at the necessary height so that everyone could enjoy the performances. The supposition may be advanced, with or without risk, that every theatrical event of the Indians, including hymns, masquerades, dances and farces, had an essentially esoteric, symbolic and ritual basis. The only extant examples which can be cited, to my knowledge, are the hymn to Tlaloc and the hymns of Netzahualcoyotl, which were neither hymns nor written by Netzahualcoyotl according to the theory of Francisco Monterde, which I share. In fact, these and other compositions have a clearly defined structure of dialogues, in the majority of cases, between a divinity and his worshipper. The following responses, taken from the hymn to Tlaloc, illustrate this theory:

1. The god appears in Mexico;[1] your banner unfurls in all directions and no one weeps.
2. I, the deity, have returned once more; I have returned again to the place which abounds in sacrifices of blood; when the day grows old there I am seen as a god.
3. Your deed is that of a noble magician; you have in truth become a being of our flesh; you have made yourself and who would dare to provoke you?
4. Certainly he who provokes me will not find himself in my favor; my ancestors seized the tigers and the serpents by the head.

It may be supposed, however, that if these compositions have come down to posterity in the form of hymns it is because "in the singing two people sang a verse and the collect answered them," and perhaps because, as the great native ceremonies were suppressed, they continued being recited in the form of monologues for their preservation through time.

---

[1] This first phrase might also be a stage direction although, contrary to the opinion of Francisco Monterde, I am inclined to consider it a part of the dialogue.

It is well known, not only historically but also through observation of the modern Mexican spirit, that the dances and festivals — controlled always by a harmonious sense of color and movement — had a particular transcendence for the ancient races of Mexico. It is worth noting that "the dance was performed almost always to the accompaniment of singing; but the song as well as the movements of those who danced were subject to the rhythm of the instruments... In the spaces between the lines of dancers buffoons usually performed, imitating other peoples in their dress or attempting with disguises of wild beasts or other animals to make the people laugh with their antics... Such were the forms of the ordinary dance; but there were many other different types in which they either performed some mystery from their religion or some event from their history or some scene relating to warfare, hunting or agriculture." The farce was, consequently, also familiar to the Indians. It is probable, however, that in them the actors themselves would improvise the dialogues and, generally, that they consisted of performances of events as they were recorded or were supposed to have happened.

In the temples of Tlalteloco and of Cholula there existed the previously mentioned earthen platforms, and the performances of which there is any record took place in Cholula during the festivals in honor of Quetzalcoatl, a deity who — because of the ebb and flow of human events — is again among us.

"This temple had a central patio where on the day of his feast great dances, celebrations and humorous interludes were held for which there was in the middle of this patio a small stage about thirty feet square, curiously whitewashed, on which they placed branches and decorated for that day with all possible neatness, surrounding it all with arches made of all types of roses and plumage, hanging at intervals many birds and rabbits and other pleasant things, where after feasting the people gathered and the performers came out and staged interludes pretending to be deaf, ill with colds, lame, blind and one-armed, all asking health of the idol as they came, the deaf answering him nonsensically; and those with colds came coughing and sneezing, and the lame came limping as they gave utterance to their misery and anguish, which made the people laugh uproariously; others came out in the trappings of vermin, some dressed as beetles and others as lizards, etc.; and

I. Cholula Pyramid

*Courtesy of the Museum of Archaeol-
ogy, History and Ethnology*

II. Cuauhtli and Ocelo-cuauhtli Dancers (*Above*)

> Tlalteloco Codex
> *Courtesy of the National Museum of Archaeology, History and Ethnology*

III. Dance of Men and Women, today called the *Matlanchines (Right)*

> Durán Atlas
> *Courtesy of the National Museum of Archaeology, History and Ethnology*

once having appeared they described their condition and, turning toward one another, played some fables [1] which the listeners enjoyed immensely because they were very clever. They pretended also to be many kinds of butterflies and birds of diverse colors, and dressed the boys from the temple in this fashion who then climbed up into an arbor which was placed there to be shot at by the priests with blowguns, which produced in defense of some and to the offense of others humorous remarks which entertained the observers greatly, all of which having concluded a great *mitote* or dance was held featuring all these persons, and all this was customarily done at the most important festivals."

These diversions were to a certain degree common to the many races which inhabited Mexico. The performance of original plays among the converted Indians of the State of Yucatan is confirmed by Fray Diego de Landa, and some of these works — like the conquest plays interspersed with song and dance — continued to exist among them at least until the second half of the nineteenth century.

---

[1] The version, or rather the copy, of Fray José de Acosta says "little flutes," which is more logical. The error stems, doubtlessly, from poor handwriting.

THE SIXTEENTH CENTURY

DURING THE YEARS which elapsed between the Conquest and the end of the sixteenth century, religious performances intensely occupied the missionaries. At first alone, and aided later by the Indian students of Tlaltelolco, they prepared in the native language *autos sacramentales* of a traditional Spanish type, adapting them to the dimensions of the auditorium and composing others which have not been preserved. The stage was also modified little by little because of the continually increasing size of the audiences attending the principal festivals and, the chapels of many naves no longer being adequately constructed for that purpose, the performances were gradually incorporated into the processions of the important occasions, being accommodated on scaffolds or platforms intended for that specific use. This contributed to the grandeur of the theatrical performances and to the broadening of their themes while affording the Indians at the same time an opportunity to display their acute decorative ability and their love of fantasy. They were themselves the actors although it seems that — as occurs in the Oriental theater — there were no actresses, those roles being performed perhaps by boys. Almost all the religious displays were comprised of the performance of passages from the Scripture, "and the *auto* of the offerings of the Magi to the Holy Child on the day of Epiphany was never omitted: the Indians considered this celebration as their own because it was the one concerning the conversion of the heathen to the Faith. In this celebration, the chroniclers note, the Indians, who were magnificent twisters of rope, brought the star from a great distance and made offerings of wax, incense, quail and doves to the manger placed in the church.

The Spanish probably introduced into Mexico City the celebration of the festivals of Corpus Christi shortly after the Conquest. There are not, however, any conclusive records in this regard before 1526. On January 9 of that year the tailors petitioned the municipal government for the designation of a site on which to construct a hermitage and a hospital for the care of the poor from which their guilds "might come forth on the day of Corpus Christi." This makes García Icazbalceta speculate that the procession existed previously. In spite of that, no clear reference is made with regard to the performances at that time. Apparently not until 1538 do the missionaries begin to practice the evangelization of the Indian masses by means of the religious theater performed in the native language. They needed time, clearly, to assimilate the native tongues to that degree. The historians, furthermore, found themselves in the same situation. The first procession of Corpus Christi which stands out most vividly is carried out in Tlaxcala on June 20, 1538, and in it the Tlaxcalans display for the first time the coat of arms presented to their city by Charles V. There was insufficient time on that day for the performances, but on Monday, June 24, 1538 — the feast of Saint John the Baptist —, the first four *autos* of which there is any record were performed on different stages: *The Annunciation of the Nativity of Saint John the Baptist Performed in the Presence of His Father Zacharias; The Annunciation of Our Lady; The Visitation of Our Lady to Saint Elizabeth,* and *The Nativity of Saint John.* Those festivals were concluded with baptisms which became the tradition for some time afterwards.

Subsequently, the Tlaxcalans themselves performed on the day of Incarnation an *auto* with the theme of Paradise which described the temptation and fall of Adam and Eve. The paraphernalia must have been unique because none of the fauna or flora of Paradise was missing and the text was faithful to the Biblical original, all of this contributing to the heightened importance of the performance. The contemporary account is dazzling. For example: "The dwelling place of Adam and Eve was so adorned as to appear like a Paradise on Earth with diverse trees with fruits and flowers, some natural and some made from feathers and gold; in the trees were many kinds of birds from owls and other birds of prey to tiny ones, and everywhere there were many parrots, and the chirping and singing were so great that at times they disturbed the performance;

I counted in a single tree fourteen large and small parrots... There were four rivers or fountains which came out of Paradise labelled Phiron, Gheon, Tigris, Euphrates; and the Tree of Life was in the middle of Paradise, and near it the Tree of the Knowledge of Good and Evil with many beautiful fruits made of gold and feathers... There were on these large rocks natural and artificial animals. On one of the artificial ones there was a boy dressed like a lion, and he was clawing and eating a deer which he had killed; the deer was real and was on a steep rock which was located between two boulders, and it was a very impressive thing."

So that nothing would be lacking, a Spanish carol considered to be the finest example of Colonial poetry was sung haphazardly at the end of that *auto*:

> *Why did she partake,*
> *The first married woman,*
> *Why did she partake*
> *Of the forbidden fruit?*
>
> *The first married woman,*
> *She and her mate,*
> *Brought God*
> *To a lowly station*
> *Because they ate*
> *The forbidden fruit.*

It is said that many of the Indians who acted in this *auto* "shed tears and were moved when Adam was exiled and placed in the world."

Contrary to the opinion of Joaquín García Icazbalceta, who maintains that "...at any rate, that carol in 1538 is the oldest example of Colonial poetry," it is not from that year. The first great Corpus Christi procession took place on June 21, 1538, and the first four performances on June 24 of the same year. The day of Incarnation falls on Easter Sunday, and the performance of the Paradise *auto* does not seem to have been prior to the first Corpus Christi procession for the chronicler states, after having described the production of the latter as being carried out in 1538: "To this end a priest living in Tlaxcallan wrote a letter to his provincial concerning the penitence and restitutions made by the Tlaxcallans during the previous Lent of 1539 and how they celebrated the feast of the Annunciation and Resurrection." Transcribed that letter adds:

"I have left the best for last, which was the celebration held by the members of the Society of Our Lady of the Incarnation, and because they could not hold it on Lent they saved it for the Wednesday of the following week... They had the paraphernalia for an *auto* dealing with the fall of our earliest ancestors set up near the doorway of the hospital." Holy Week having fallen in the last days of March of the year 1539, it can be deduced that the festival of Incarnation was postponed for a week so that carol, therefore, dated from 1539.

According to Fray Motolinia the news of the peace treaty between France and Spain was received a little after Lent in 1539. Bernal Díaz mentions the same fact as having occurred in 1538 but it may have been toward the last part of the year, and the news, at any rate, arrived in Tlaxcala later. The Tlaxcalans decided to see what the Spanish and the Mexicans would do regarding the matter in order to make their own decision concerning the local celebration of the event. Between the end of March and the beginning of April, 1539, there was performed in Mexico City a *Conquest of Rhodes*. "...In Mexico City great feasts and banquets were held as a result of the peace agreement arranged between our Christian Emperor and Master of glorious memory and King Francis of France at the time of the meetings held at Aigues-Mortes... after this, in the middle of the same central plaza on another day, arose the city of Rhodes in its entirety with its towers and battlements and embrasures and ramparts surrounded by a wall and as natural as the true Rhodes, and with one hundred commanders with their rich emblems all of gold and many pearls, and many of them mounted like gentlemen on horseback with their lances and shields, and others riding stiff-legged in order to break lances and shields, and others on foot with their blunderbusses, and as Captain General and Grand Master of Rhodes was Marquis Cortés, and they brought four ships with their masts and foresails and yardarms and sails, and they were so real that some persons marvelled at seeing them go sailing through the middle of the plaza and around it three times while firing the artillery with Indians on board dressed as Dominican friars as when they come from Castile plucking some hens, and other friars were fishing, but let us leave the ships and their artillery and fittings and let me tell of how two companies of Turks were placed in a very realistic Turkish ambush with very rich clothes of silk and carmine and scarlet with much gold and rich hoods as they

wear them in their land and all on horseback and anxious to make
an assault and carry off certain shepherds with their cattle who were
grazing near a fountain, and one of the shepherds tending them
fled and informed the Grand Master of Rhodes because the Turks
were taking away the cattle and shepherds, and the commanders
set out (unclear in the original: "and as their captain the Marquis
del Valle, their king") and these and the ones who took the booty
of cattle attack each other, and other squadrons of Turks come
down from another direction upon Rhodes and set upon the commanders who took many of the Turks and even set loose bulls to
dispatch them..." The Tlaxcalans having seen this, "they determined to perform the Conquest of Jerusalem, which future arrangement God grant may be fulfilled in our times, and to make it
more solemn they agreed to leave it for the day of Corpus Christi."
This day (June 5) having arrived, the performance was carried out.
Together with the *Conquest of Rhodes,* this *Conquest of Jerusalem,*
a similar imitation of warfare, offers the uniqueness of being a primitive example of the mass theater directed recently by Vsevolod
Mayerhold in Russia.

"In Tlaxcallan, in the city which they have begun to build anew,
in a low flat place they left a large pleasant plaza, on which they
had built Jerusalem above some houses which are being constructed
for the municipal government, on a site where the buildings already
reached one story in height; they levelled it all and filled it with
earth and made five towers; one for worship in the center and
larger than the rest, and the other four at the four corners; they
were closed off by a very turreted wall, and the towers were also
crenelated and festive, with many windows and festive arches all
filled with roses and flowers... Then the army of Spain began to
surround Jerusalem and, passing in front of the Corpus Christi, it
crossed the plaza and established its encampment on the right side.
It was quite long in entering because there were many people
divided into three squadrons... Having passed among these, and
having set up their headquarters, they were followed by the army
of New Spain which entered from the opposite side divided into
ten companies, each one clad in the costumes they employ in
warfare; these were very pleasant to behold, and in Italy and
in Spain if they could see them they would be quite satisfied. They
wore the finest rich plumages, shields and bucklers because all

those who participated in this *auto* were lords and men of importance who refer to each other as *Teuhpiltin*."

The Pope, Cardinals, Bishops, Emperor of Spain, Kings of
France and Hungary were there in full regalia. A fictitious Count
of Benavente commanded the Spanish troops; the heathen were
commanded by an apocryphal Antonio de Mendoza, then Viceroy
of New Spain, and an Indian who played the role of the Great
Sultan of Babylonia and Tetrarch of Jerusalem and imitated Hernán
Cortés. There was an exchange of messages between Emperor and
Pope, prayers, and angels and apostles —Santiago, Saint Hippolytus
and Saint Michael— gleamed in the *auto* to temper in their fire
the Christian souls of the conquerors. The *auto* is attributed to
Fray Motolinia, the guardian of the convent of Tlaxcala and
director of those festivals in which there were three additional
autos: The Temptations of Our Lord, in which a consort of
demons and a Lucifer who was "a very deformed hermit" were
the central figures; *The Preaching of Saint Francis to the Birds,*
from which the classic wolf was not missing, and which was
concluded with a fire which featured a Hell complete with spectators who believed that the damned were burning because of
sins of intemperance, and *The Sacrifice of Adam,* "which because
it was brief and the hour already late can only be called entertaining."

Although no specific date is known, between 1535 and 1548
there was performed in Mexico City, in the chapel of San José
de Naturales —constructed by Fray Pedro de Gante and considered to be the cathedral of the Indians— an *auto* called *The
Last Judgement,* composed in the Mexican language by the mis-
sionary Fray Andrés de Olmos. The period of time specified is
during the governorship of Antonio de Mendoza and the term of
office of Bishop Juan de Zumárraga, both of whom appear to have
attended the performance.

It is to be supposed that the Indians, who loaned to some of
those processions their animal costumes and their dances, might
have added also some of their pagan rites just as they fused their
vision and their symbols to the architectural constructions of the
Colonial period in order to preserve them. This would explain,
taken together with the religious inflexibility of the times, why
Bishop Zumárraga added, in a second edition of the treatise by

Dionisio Cartujano concerning the manner in which processions should be performed with reverence and devotion —printed apparently in 1544 or 1545— an appendix in which he vehemently prohibited such interjections together with all else which might be categorized as dishonorable and pagan.

"...And it is a thing of great disrespect and shame that before the Holy Sacrament men should go about with masks and in women's attire, dancing and jumping about with immodest and lascivious motions... Those who do it, and those who order it, and even those who permit it, who might otherwise avoid it and do not, will have to look to another than Fray Juan de Zumárraga to pardon them... And it would not be with slight prejudice to their souls and to doctrine to those who teach this to these natives. And all of this, even if this vain and profane and licentious practice is tolerated in other lands among other peoples, should in no way be permitted and encouraged among the natives of this new Church."

The innocence of the Indians was doubtlessly another fabulous pyramid upon whose ruins he urged Spain to erect a medieval and Christian church.

Nevertheless, it is thought that the Bishop alone condemned the profanity and dishonesty for "according to another writer there was a religious named Las Casas who wrote a farce entitled *The Last Judgement* which he dedicated to Zumárraga and had printed in 1546." At any rate, this prohibition reduced the processional festivities to strictly religious ceremonies until June 3, 1548, at which time the Bishop died and the office was left vacant and the city government again permitted performances and dances on the day of Corpus. According to one contemporary chronicler, however, when all was in readiness for the procession an exceptionally hard morning rain prevented the procession from starting. The city council, fearful of the unusual shower which it took as clear evidence of divine disapproval, revoked the permit for the celebration and decided to leave in effect Fray Juan de Zumárraga's decree for as long as his position was vacant.

The preceding prohibition and several matters of importance which required the work of the religious and the attention of government officials, particularly the opening of the University on January 25, 1553, cooled the enthusiasm for the theater greatly.

IV. The Coyote Dance
(*Above*)

Codex Borbonicus
Courtesy of the National Library of Mexico

V. Symbolic Priestly Dance
called the *Volador (Left)*

Codex Borbonicus
Courtesy of the National Library of Mexico

Nothing more is heard of it until 1565 when the Ecclesiastical Council, in spite of everything, gave a different opinion, stating that on May 18 of each year it would give "a jewel of gold or silver of a value up to thirty escudos for the best performance or script that might be performed on the day of Corpus." On the other hand, the municipal council offered in its turn, for the same purpose, "jewels," a term apparently applied generally to all prizes regardless of their nature.

The marvelous production of the presbyter Fernán González de Eslava, the only specialized writer and almost the only author of the sixteenth century whose works are preserved, thanks to Joaquín García Icazbalceta who had them reprinted in 1877, date from between 1567 and 1600.

González de Eslava was certainly a Spaniard, perhaps an Andalusian, and was probably from Seville. In spite of this, his *Spiritual Colloquies* are filled with what today we call local color, and often include expressions in Nahuatl and make reference to purely local events in New Spain. There can be perceived in some of them a great attention to Mexican things, which was quite profound because he was a theologian in his time, and a rebelliousness against the classical structure of the *autos sacramentales*. González Pedrozo defines them as dramatic works in one act in praise of the Mystery of the Eucharist. Eslava composes colloquies of up to seven acts in length, and does not limit himself only to praise of the Mystery. His sixteen *Spiritual Colloquies* embrace several themes, always possessing a religious purpose and an allegorical intent which are frequently impossible to stage, but which are generally motivated by a spirit of innovation. The most original in my view, and the one with least defects, is *The Divine Handiwork*. In the rest, although the verse is simple and frequently elegant, there is a certain aura of deliberateness, of dependence not on the divine but on the human and the powerful. This is true because the author does not possess the talent necessary to do more than is required of him. He has another equally estimable obstinacy: he is inclined toward allegorical figures which reproached the critics of the Spanish literary renascence scandalously; he employs the fool or simpleton, "only to inspire laughter," as he himself says. There slips occasionally into his works a criticism of contemporary things which at times approaches satire, such as when he speaks of the poets, in *Colloquy XVI* (*Concerning the Forest in which Our Lord has His Birds and Animals*):

Doña Murmuración to Remoquete: "You are becoming poetic; you will earn little as a poet, for there are more than there is dung: look for another profession: it will be worth more to you to spend a day making bricks than a year writing sonnets."

He inserts in passing in his colloquies little reports concerning the performances in vogue and, without being the best because he is by himself, he is doubtlessly of great importance from the historical, literary and linguistic point of view. Joaquín García Icazbalceta says that "although defects may be noticed in the *Colloquies,* particularly if one falls into the error of judging them according to the standards of taste prevalent in our times, it is not difficult to point out, on the other hand, merits which more than compensate for the defects; furthermore, they constitute a very important monument in the history of Mexican literature or Spanish literature, which are one in the same." I would dare to suggest, however, that they are not the same thing.

Because of the prizes offered by the Ecclesiastical Council and the municipal government, and the abundance of poets so roundly criticized by Eslava, there is nothing until 1574, when the presbyter Juan Pérez Ramírez, a Mexican who received fifty pesos in cash yearly for keeping a list of holy performances, composes a play entitled *Spiritual Marriage Between the Shepherd Peter and the Mexican Church,* which was staged on December 8 of that year in the Cathedral on the occasion of the investiture of Archbishop Pedro Moya de Contreras. This work, entirely allegorical, exists in manuscript form in the National Library of Mexico.

About the same time, González de Eslava must have composed and had performed his Colloquy entitled *Concerning the Consecration of Pedro Moya de Contreras, Archbishop of Mexico* (Number Three), which seems to me superior to the work of Pérez Ramírez.

Theatrical performances most assuredly dealt, apart from processions, with the principal events of the day. Nor is it too much to assume that other types besides religious ones were being introduced slowly into the theater. Contemporary criticism certainly aspired to such a forum; at the least government, if not politics, passed through the narrow portal of criticism, which is so close that one must leave something behind on passing through it. In this regard there exists the precedent that after the performance of a play by Pérez Ramírez, an *entremés* in which the tax collectors were satirized, the result was the censure of the Archbishop by both Viceroy and municipal government and the imprisonment of Juan de Victoria, who performed in the play with the choir-boys, González de Eslava, who ordered it, and Francisco de Terrazas, who was called "a great poet" and was the alleged author of lines critical of the authorities.

On the ocassion of the arrival of the relics sent by Pope Gregory XIII to the Jesuits of the province of Mexico, a great festival was held in 1578 in which there was a procession of symbols and students, dances and recitations and, on the first six days of the first week, holy performances. Among these figured one particularly brilliant event, a five act tragedy entitled *The Triumph of the Saints*. In it were "the persecution of Diocletian and the prosperity which followed with the empire of Constantine," and Saint Sylvester, Constantine, Dacian the messenger, Cromatius the president, Saint Peter, Saint Dorotheus, Saint John and Saint Gorgonius, two knights named Albinus and Olympus, a nuncio and his secretary, two bailiffs, the Church, Faith, Hope, Charity, Gentility, Idolatry and Cruelty, all of which appeared on stage. This work was performed by students, and it produced a greatly salubrious and pious effect on the audience. By an anonymous author, it is thought that several people collaborated in writing it. It is contained in a volume which is in Madrid which also has "The Letter from Father Pedro de Morales of the Company of Jesus to the Very Reverend Father Everardo Mercuriano, General of the same Company, in which an account is given of the Festival which was held in this incomparable City of Mexico in this seventy-eighth year of the arrival of the Holy Relics which our Very Holy Father Gregory XIII sent to them." (Printed in Mexico City in 1579 by Antonio Ricardo). The cover sheet of the tragedy is found on page 109, and it is probable, because the book has 199 pages, that this work covers ninety of them.

The Third Mexican Council, held in the year 1585, confirmed in part the prohibition of Zumárraga, proscribing from the temples "dances, profane performances and songs even on the day of Our Lord's Nativity, in the festival of Corpus and other similar events."

However, the Council itself added: "But if some sacred story
or other holy and useful things for the soul are to be performed, or
some sacred hymns to be sung, they should be presented one month
previously to the Bishop so that they may be examined and approved by him" (Book III, Item 18-1). Apart from this the theater
remained free outside the churches, and the *autos sacramentales,*
originally performed in them by ecclesiastical persons according
to Eslava, went out into the streets, there to undergo changes which
would make them more worldly when staged by professional actors.
Concerning the latter there is, in spite of everything, nothing but
silence. It is known that in the year 1588, when the Inquisition
formulated the censure of theatrical works which were performed,
"a fifty peso gratuity was given to a boy who performed well in
the play." And there is nothing more until that date.

Isolated remarks have been found, like the following, which
establish a vague contact with several authors and actors: "1586—
Alonso de Buenrostro, author of the plays of Corpus for that year
in Mexico City."

Apparently between 1589 and 1594 the scholar Arias de Villalobos, who was subpoenaed by the municipal government on June
9, 1589, for not having fulfilled the contract for the festival of
Corpus, was employed as author and exclusive empresario. Wishing
perhaps to enter again into favor, the scholar went on August 29,
1594, to the council to solicit the position of official author to
the city with a subsidy of two thousand pesos per year, an agreement under which he would obligate himself to take charge of the
festivals of Corpus during the entire week and the week of Saint
Hippolytus, the patron saint of New Spain, together with performances based on new scripts. Villalobos was unsuccessful in spite
of the fact that in the minutes of the city government dated February 13, 1595, his proposition was accepted with only the author-
ization of the Viceroy awarding him the two thousand pesos
lacking. A reconsideration was required when Gonzalo de Riancho,
who referred to himself as a playwright, presented to the municipal
council a petition similar to the one of Arias de Villalobos (March
2, 1595). He offered to do the plays for fifteen hundred pesos, and
he added that such was his "proper profession and livelihood,"
and that he had come to Mexico from Havana "with a company
of people for the said performances," bringing "plays and holy

dialogues written in Spain by the most famous men, among them admirable works, all of which are better than those proposed by the said Villalobos." He evidently had at his disposal actors and, although there are no other data, he is to be believed because the city council accepted his proposal and, consequently, he produced the plays from that year on. It is certain that he was not paid the fifteen hundred pesos, receiving only nine hundred ninety, for after Corpus he requested a "gratuity for expenses incurred," claiming that he had spent more than three thousand pesos on that endeavor and, in spite of the fact that he supposedly "composed and had studied a great play of the greatest authority... which deals with the conquest of this New Spain and great City of Mexico," the city council does not appear to have been swayed, for it is not recorded that so much as a reply was sent. He deserved it, doubtlessly, because he set such a low price on his talents. Nevertheless, it seems that the performance of that *Conquest* on August 13 of each year, the anniversary of the taking of the city by Hernán Cortés, was a tradition for some time.

Elsewhere, it appears that in July of 1595 an actor named Navijo requested financial aid for a *Play concerning the Conquest*. In 1596 the performances were again the responsibility of Riancho, but in 1597 preference was given to others with whom a price of six hundred pesos was agreed to for the play and three *entremeses*. This must have been inspired by the claims of Riancho, who finally received fifteen hundred pesos for the plays in 1598. In 1599, on the other hand, the city council had no funds for the celebration of Corpus Christi and there was no play, at least none of a municipal nature. If there was one, the corresponding expenses were paid by the Society for Plays, which came into existence in 1597 near the Hospital of Jesus, which was founded by Hernán Cortés in a building belonging to Francisco de León.

As the sixteenth century came to a close, the Franciscan Fray Francisco de Gamboa, founder of the religious fraternity of Our Lady of Solitude at the chapel of San José, began the pantomime performances of the stages of the Passion, which were done on Friday during the sermon and which were to enjoy popularity up to the present time when contemporary practice has abandoned them to the exclusive domain of the rural areas. Among the most typical may be cited those which accompanied the sermons of the Seizure, the Three Falls, and the Descent.

The introduction into the Sunday service of the *neixcuitilli* —examples or models in Nahuatl— by Fray Juan de Torquemada, who composed some of them while others were written by his master of theatrical arts Fray Juan Bautista, "a great Nahuatlist and fecund writer" who warmly predicted the great religious utility of the theater in 1599, coincided with the other performances.

Besides the performances of *autos* in Mexico City and Tlaxcala, there appear reports of others carried out in Etla (Oaxaca), one of which ended in 1575 with the unexpected theatrical effect of the collapse of a portico and the subsequent death of one hundred twenty people including that of the guardian of the convent, Fray Alonso de la Anunciación, not to mention numerous injured.

From the opening of the trial by the Holy Inquisition of Antonio López, "who plays and sings in dramas and is a native of Seville," for "suspected Jewish sympathies" and "abetting of Jews," there comes a true three act play: the rope torture, the rack torture and burning at the stake, which is set in the seventeenth century because the trial was closed in 1600.

Nothing, in summation, was now lacking in the theater.

Also in the sixteenth century, the wagons used so much in Spain figured in processions and performances; Eslava mentions them in the stage directions to some of his colloquies. Likewise, it may or may not be believed, depending or not upon whether certain statements are accepted, that Gutierre de Cetina, the hero of the madrigal who came to Mexico City in 1546, wrote here a book of morality plays in prose and verse and another of profane plays; that Juan de la Cueva, who came between 1574 and 1577, did not write his plays here; and that Luis de Belmonte Bermúdez, the author of *The Preaching Devil,* was twice in our country, "where not being able to forget the savory ambrosia of the Muses he wrote many plays, some of which are in print, and the life of the Patriarch Ignacio de Loyola in Spanish verse." (Prologue by Master Juan Bermúdez y Alfaro to the unpublished poem of Bermúdez, "The Hispálica." Quoted from Menéndez y Pelayo.) Finally, it may be accepted that, as stated by Eugenio de Salazar in his

Epistle and Balbuena in his *The Grandeur of Mexico,* the tragic and comic genres and theatrical spectacles were cultivated with a certain intensity and perfection in Mexico. In short, a promise is made to the following century.

However...

INTERLUDE

WITH TWENTY YEARS of his youth in the sixteenth century and the remainder of his life in the seventeenth, there arises toward the end of the former the inscrutable figure of Juan Ruiz de Alarcón. Alarcón is situated between two lands just as he stands between two centuries. His contemporaries classify him as a *criollo,* and his critics at that time, because they could find no better outlet for their candor, characterize him with the adjective foreign. Spain, however, has made for him a place of homage on its enormous Olympus, and European encyclopedias parade him in their résumés of the Spanish theater. Ambitions and ancestry are Spanish in Alarcón's life and, in general, the courtiers and ladies who come to life in his works are Spanish as well. It is true, on the other hand, that European and American men of letters with subtle and attentive perception have discovered in him details which place him under the emblem of Mexico; they have found that reflections different from the Castilian and expressions of an inner nature in which the rustic and haughty egalitarianism of the Iberian fabric are not present. He has an inner nature in which there is, unlike the sonority of his forebears, a new form of expression: silence. And it is true that Alarcón possesses all of that. But not all that alone.

In spite of the loftiness and brilliance of the diverse opinions proffered on both sides, it is still not impertinent to ask if Alarcón belongs definitively to Mexico or Spain.

"Between a genius and his time there exists the relationship of the strong to the weak, of the old man to the youth." Nietzsche claims. This could explain and, at first glance, make of Juan Ruiz de Alarcón a Mexican, but this is explosive material heaped up

VI.   Juan Ruiz de Alarcón y Mendoza

by our own theatrical poverty during the sixteenth century. However, Nietzsche himself also states, with less arbitrariness and more correctness: "Beauty is no accident. The beauty of a race, a family, its grace, its perfection in all respects, is acquired laboriously: it is, like genius, the final result of the accumulated travail of generations." If, after reading this statement, one discovers the Juan Ruiz de Alarcón who is only one of several highlights of the Spanish theater, then one assuredly does not encounter the Juan Ruiz de Alarcón who is the supreme figure of the Mexican theater.

Setting out on the unlikely route of the hypothesis it may be ascertained that the sobriety, the reticence, the discretion which are reputed Mexican attributes of Juan Ruiz, together with the gray tonality of which Pedro Henríquez Ureña speaks, are subject to another explanation: his daily life. From the same source may emanate his meticulous observation and mature judgement. Did Alarcón play as a child? Did he fall in love as a young man? He was not in a position to waste his fortune in his younger days with the same brilliant disorderliness of those who were children and young men with him. His perennially filled larder must have weighed heavily upon him, that way of life which he could not dispose of slowly while contemplating and observing those who ran to and fro and had their love affairs. Offended and often assaulted, perhaps daily, he was obliged to mistrust, to analyze in each man who might draw near to him the net amount of cruelty, of lack of conscience, or of goodness. Frequently rejected, he subjects himself in a disciplinary fashion to reticence, perhaps to his own avarice, outside of his plays.

He was courteous, but it is not known whether he was because he was Mexican or merely intelligent. Courtesy is the strength of the weak and the perfection of the strong. Or at least it was formerly. He expresses himself with circumspection, but perhaps out of fear of calling the attention of others too much to his unfortunate back, and this feeling permeates the brevity of his sentences. He reworks and polishes his works, in whose perfection there is the secret of the counterweight to his involuntary physical deformities. He makes the trip, in short, to his own promised land as comfortably as he can on the same steed on which other men go toward the extreme that frequently does not exist in them. He pretends not to attract attention and, naturally, attracts it. Accursed attention.

His theater is out of tune in "this world which in the works of the Spanish dramatists comes alive and shakes itself giddily, knotting and reknotting conflicts as in a complex dance set." How can it freely be stated that he never wished to break with understatement and restraint and give free expression to the great Spanish voice which reverberated inside him? It is possible that he did not express himself in Lopesque terms for the same reason that prevented him from running and playing earlier: so as not to set off laughter, that savage human explosion. An intelligent man in that physical condition imposes incredible prohibitions and disciplines upon himself which transform the normal mind because they are so terrible and puerile. At any rate, in his way, Juan Ruiz de Alarcón doubtlessly followed the Socratic path. I could, in my turn, continue along this same path which has already been adequately described, but it is not necessary.

Discarding the theory of the environment as a creative force, there must have predominated in Alarcón his long European ancestry —he did have a heritage— and that Hispanic awareness of life which was nurtured by centuries of direct evolution, which flourished almost grotesquely in the Golden Age while making of Spain a phenomenon of artistic fecundity overshadowing the phenomenal fecundity of the world at that time, occupied a vast expanse of his moral and intellectual life. It is demonstrated, furthermore, in his journey to Spain to search for the future and his departure from the colonies. It is proven specifically by his obvious status as a Renaissance man.

Twenty years of life in Mexico which began by adding the hues to the basic color and ended by being replaced by them, were sufficient, however, to make of Alarcón a notable example of the modern artistic personality. Alarcón, a Spanish color combined with Mexican hues, thus acquired that intellectual and moral aspect which kept him from receiving the esteem of his great Spanish contemporaries. It is known that with the exception of Lope, whom such a disciple had no choice but to praise, the others never forgave him for anything; "the enormous wave which swelled against Alarcón was unleashed by the attacks of an unrestrained group of musketeers in order to cause the failure of each one of his works; it was a conspiracy of unhealthy passions undertaken to vex, satirize and ridicule that superior man..." Because of that same combination of hues —as with everything else produced by the fusion of races or customs— he achieved the status of being more universal, escaping many of the hereditary conventions of the pure breeds. Viewed from this angle, he seems to be something more than a Mexican: rather a Mexicanist, a foreshadowing of what Mexicans will become in the future. I note in passing that if he had heirs racially he lacked on the other hand successors in the Mexican theater.

A creator of dramatic genres and customs because of this uniqueness, which of course he projected consciously through his silence, and because of his parsimony —only a platform of twenty-six plays next to the gigantic dais of his contemporaries— he must be one of the most complete examples of theatrical modernity together with Molière. The latter probably becomes acquainted with his *The Truth Suspected* through *The Liar* of Corneille, and finds there the definition of his own intentions, the true orientation of his talent and the renovation of the French theater. The statement is attributed to Molière, nevertheless, that among essentially productive men and peoples the first importation is translated into the standard, is a discovery of their own elements and is immediately applied. Voltaire attributes the fecund and subtle life of Molière to an acquaintance with *The Liar,* and Molière confesses to Boileau that without it he would not have written *The Misanthrope.* But if Poquelin had not been Molière, being French proportionally might have saved him. If he had not been French, he probably would not have been much more than an unimportant translator.

Alarcón doubtlessly had within him all that was required to be who he was: he was linked to the classics by study that was more impassioned than normal, and his life, which had no value in the present, could be concentrated into a fair compromise for the future. Life is in him not art or energy, as in a Leonardo or a Goethe, but is contemplation and work. If he has no lyrical enthusiasm, he possesses clarity and correctness of form and spiritual convictions controlled by the supersensibility of a sick man: he has a perfect moral ear and, moreover, he is honorable. He has the same reasons for not being venomous that motivate the common man. He is not spiteful because he is sad. He is not brutal because he is ironic. He possesses, in fact, his own concentrated power and

an obsession with uprightness and interior nobility which inspire
him to create a part of modern morality. If his imagination had
been more poetic than humanistic, he would have been able to
write marvelous things instead of admirable things. "An artist
with a classical spirit, the term being taken in the sense of a sober
and contemplative artist, he is also of that bent because of his
fondness for the literature of Latium and because of his frequently
indicated affinity with the sober and pensive muse of Terence."

Beyond the fact that his studies brought him close to the
ancients, the reform that he brought to the theater was certainly
caused by another factor, and I believe that it is found in Mexico
and in the prevalent theatrical backwardness. It may be assumed
that in his childhood, and at the beginning of his youth, he followed
closely the performances that were held in New Spain, and that the
constant presence of the theological and cardinal vices and virtues
in the *autos* presented caused to germinate within him the idea of
humanizing them by placing them in persons of flesh and blood.
Everyone profited from this change, including the vices and virtues,
because they became so active and interesting in men that they did
not pass in Heaven and Hell for mere collector's items.

With regard to Alarcón —insulted and misunderstood by his
contemporaries in Spain— he achieved, because of all these reasons,
the difficult glory of remaining forever in the history of the theater
in Spanish, and he is the only Renaissance man in the letters of
post-Cortesian Mexico.

THE SEVENTEENTH CENTURY

IT SEEMS that after the passing of the sixteenth century, "a heroic period in our letters," lyric and dramatic poetry are intensified; that the theater, master of a more progressive population which is more knowledgeable about life, is destined to be the answer to the need for expression of a race in the process of unification. The simple and impressive medieval themes are, on the other hand, a proper basis for a national expression of criticism and for an ideal. Nations and peoples always strive toward expression and one hundred years heap up customs, traditions and the need for change. Nevertheless, here the rule is broken. It does not happen this way, and precisely from that time forward it begins not to happen that way for centuries.

Some still great flowers, but mainly withering ones from the fabulous Spanish literature, Gongorism and *conceptismo,* are exported to America. New colonists, they develop irresistibly here, they conquer the field of poetry and prose, and the chargers of *culteranismo* graze on the very steps of sacred history and oratory. The indescribable erudite poetry —which has returned again to preside over our most recent literary movements and from which we are scarcely beginning to liberate ourselves— catches fire in Mexico. All the poets burn in it as did the most insignificant Latin rhymer, even the circumspect and balanced Carlos de Sigüenza y Góngora. Latin and pedantry are the password for admission to the period of intellectual drought which is begun. Creative enthusiasm is no longer poetic but literary.

In principle all decadence is renovation. In the activity of a people or of men there are always known and unknown forces, pressing and latent ones, chosen and disdained ones. When only the latter ones remain they should be used solely so as not to obstruct their consumption, and they display themselves with such vigor and so colorfully that there is not a single dying man who does not believe himself saved by merely wielding them. In principle, likewise, all decadence is ingenious. The ingenuity of an initial cycle is active and fecund; that of a decadent one is multiple and selective. If the former explains, the latter comprehends. And the message of culture never goes beyond this point. A genius launches it in the East and another catches it, now enormous, crepuscular and more fiery than at the beginning, in the West.

If we did not have Góngora in Mexico to justify a similar movement —a revolution without revolutionary goals— at least we enjoyed a fanfare of Gongorism, and with such verve that "when it had almost passed out of its region of origin because of the restorers of good taste, in Mexico imitating Góngora continued apace." Our formidable acoustic capacity, which lends such varied forms to any outcry and so prolongs it, initiates its hegemony. This is the primordial Mexican vice. From that moment on decadence will be more appealing to the mind of the new race than plenitude because of what it imagines concerning indolence, softness and elegance, and because it is the state cultivated to the point of atmosphere of the ancient Mexican people. The Spanish produced two great things in Mexico: decadence and renovation. The first is doubtlessly the more grandiose of the two.

On the other hand, to complement the blind activity of lyric letters and their inane fruits, painting and architecture are developed: physicians, geologists, geographers, geodesists, astronomers, mineralogists and, in another area, humanists and philosophers are protected by the moral climate of New Spain as historians had been formerly.

But the seventeenth century, particularly during the first half, appears to be monumentally empty, sumptuously empty, in the matter of literature. A period of respite and of expectation, a subconscious lurking of new stars for lyric poetry and for dramatic poetry, it is not even an interesting blank page. The first literary museum in Mexico, Gongorism collects pieces whose condition is abnormality, whether on a large or small scale. Deeds are done which terminate in madness, monsters of originality with seven heads are hunted and, worse yet, writing is done as it was then:

by the bucketful. Voyages are taken to the North Pole, to the South Pole and to the North Africa of literature. All forms are practiced, dressed well or badly in Latin: twenty varieties of sonnets, *décimas,* royal octaves, acrostics, anagrams, *centones,* labyrinths... The serious thing about this period of Freudian affiliation is that no spirit controls that intense labor of farmers gone mad who employ, with minute propriety, their implements of fecundation in an imagined or barren land. "Uselessly would one search in the copious legacy which those laborious literati bequeath us for something which might reveal to us the states of mind which tie together the drama of life. How can one explain such a singular phenomenon? Were those men perhaps protected by a stoic sensibility which rendered them invulnerable to the debilities and miseries of our poor race beset by desires and insatiable aspirations? The answer is difficult. For our part, we shall limit ourselves to pointing out this strange deficiency in our literary history which had to produce that uniformity of artificial lucubrations, all traced from the same pattern and activated by the same mechanism, with few exceptions.

There being no valid reason for the theater to have escaped the influence which propels it, even within similar areas there must have abounded writers of *loas, autos,* colloquies and even dramas. However, their works are either worthless and are quickly consumed or are confiscated and prohibited by the ecclesiastical authorities since thought was frequently exposed and confiscated in the customs houses of holy censorship. In any case, the works of religious propaganda do not seem to have attained great brilliance either. The processional festivities continue, doubtlessly, as well as the sacred and courtly celebrations which so frequently included dramas. In the processions the giants and the crippled devil, whose existence in the previous century Eslava confirms, are still featured.

> *Do you know whom that woman resembles?*
> *That crippled devil*
> *who ambles about on festival day.*

Only in 1618, however, does an author appear fleetingly: "1618.— Francisco Maldonado, playwright, agreed with the Archbishop and Council of the Cathedral of Mexico City to do the plays 'which must be performed in our cathedral during the week of celebrations which are to be held concerning the Immaculate Conception of Mary... Mother of God.' He received four hundred pesos of a total of six hundred on the sixth of December. On the eighteenth of January of 1619 a draft was issued for the other two hundred which were paid on the twenty-first. Then the majordomo of the enterprise hurried to the Council requesting that a draft be issued for the six hundred pesos for his acquittal, and the agreement which resulted from his petition was as follows: 'Saturday March 2 of 1619 a. d. This petition having been seen by Your Servants the Dean and Council of this Holy Church, they stated that inasmuch as the players did not fulfill their obligation with regard to performing new plays, as well as on festival day, it is requested that His Eminence see fit to have his former decree suspended.' Archives of the Cathedral of Mexico City."

A *Play about the Kings,* written in the native language at the beginning of the seventeenth century by Agustín de la Fuente and translated in the nineteenth century by the scholar Francisco del Paso y Troncoso, and a *Colloquy concerning the Recent Conversion and Baptism of the Last Four Kings of Tlaxcala in New Spain* by Cristóbal Gutiérrez de Luna, "a *criollo* of Mexico," dated in Tlaxcala in the year of 1619 and included in a volume which contains a "Record of the/Matter of the Angels Life of the Archbishop Don/P° Moya de Contreras Patriarch of the In/dies and other Curious Things," can be mentioned in the first half of the seventeenth century. The last manuscript mentioned is presently found at the University of Texas, in the collection of Genaro García, and a photostatic copy is in the National Library of Mexico where I was able to read it.

It is believable "that in 1621 there were in Mexico three companies of actors who performed in two different theaters plays from Castile with a preference for those written here, and they were not favorably received." This is taken from the description of Mexico made by that scholar Arias de Villalobos in his poem entitled "Mercury," which he addressed to the Viceroy Marquis de Montes Claros "extolling the fortunate day" on which the latter arrived to rule in New Spain, which was published in 1623 together with a "Narrative of Royal Obedience" dedicated to Philip IV. (Printshop of Diego Garrido, Mexico City, 1623):

For people who are fond of high living,
Two housefuls of professional joymakers and
Performers of plays which have travelled about
But were written here...

Two notes concerning the second and third verses state: "1.—Two different playhouses and three companies of actors. 2.—They performed plays from Castile; those from here are unsuccessful."

Otherwise in the seventeenth century "there were dramas at court and plays were performed in the name of the Viceroys, at the swearing in of the sovereign and on other solemn days."

The theatrical performances were not limited to the capital of the Viceroyalty, they were done at various places in the country: "1645.—From the ledger of the majordomo of the parish of Santa Prisca de Taxco: To put on the play and the *loa* of the songs which were sung on the day of Our Lady, six and one-half pesos.—For the setting up of the stage to the carpenter, and for shoes that were given to the boys, and for tacks and nails and pins and for other things which were necessary, twenty-eight pesos and three farthings.—Parish Archives."

It appears that in the *auto de fe* performed in the Volador plaza on April 11, 1649, under the rule of Marcos Torres y Rueda, Bishop of Yucatán and twentieth Viceroy of New Spain, there was doing penance — and not in effigy — the author of a play entitled *At the End Glory is Sung,* which had the plot of *The Deceiver of Seville* according to information which I owe to Luis González Obregón, and whose principal character, as pointed out by José Martínez Aranda, was a Jew and, therefore, constituted a major offense. The volume of the archive of the Inquisition in which this trial and the play which prompted it were contained was lost during the last century.

The presence of professional actors and the theatrical habits of the people are found, however vaguely, in the newspaper accounts of the time. Unfortunately, the only examples available now are excerpts of the following sort:

July 3, 1650.—"The Viceroy Don Luis Enríquez de Guzmán made his public entry into this City on the twenty first... and he was brought in this way to the corner of the street of Santo Domingo, where the City is accustomed to receiving the Viceroys, and

in it was an arch with two sides with the legend of Proteus...
arriving at this place an actor explained to him what had been
painted... And they returned to the Cathedral, and before he entered
the fable of Hercules which was painted on the doorway was explained to him by an actor together with its title: poetry and *loa*
composed by Father Matías de Bocanegra, of the Company of Jesus."

1651.—"June 8 (Day of Corpus), they placed the monstrance in
the usual location for the play and the Viceroy, Court, Tribunals
and some canons witnessed it."

1653.—(January.) "Festival of Our Lady of the Conception...
on the following day there was a play in the silversmith's shop,
and on Tuesday bulls at the small plaza of the Schools, and on
Wednesday there came forth from them an elaborate masquerade
with some fables and carts, and among them the City of Troy,
which was burned in view of the Viceroy, and the abduction of
Helen." Week of Corpus.—"There was a stage where the play was
performed to the left of the platform, where the Holy Sacrament
was."—August 3 (arrival of Archbishop Marcelo López de Azcona)
"the procession continued up to the doorway of the Cathedral, and
in it was explained by an actor named Medina the fable of... which
were the figures in the arch."

1654.—"The King is forty-nine years of age.—Wednesday, the
last day of Easter Resurrection, on the eighth of April of 1654,
the Viceroy Duke of Alburquerque... and the dancing party and
play continued on the following day, Thursday, after Prayers."

1656.—(February.) "The Dedication of the Cathedral (festivities
began on Tuesday 1st)... 13 of February, and the Vicereine celebrated the festival of the Most Holy... the Sunday of the week
following this dedication, at two in the afternoon, they finished the
Most Holy Sacrament... the Tuesday of the week referred to
the Our Father was ended because at two o'clock the Viceroy, Court,
and Tribunals and all the retinue came to see a bizarre drama performed which had been prepared by the students entering the Royal
University."

1658.—"Celebration of the birthday of the Prince Próspero.—
Thursday 28 of November, they say that our Lord the Prince was

one year old... until the Viceroy returned to the palace, where that afternoon the Court was held and the ladies of nobility of the retinue attended the drama and dancing party which the Viceroy had ordered."

1660.—"Mexico City celebrated the festival of Corpus this year as usual, and the stage for the drama was not set up in the cemetery of the Cathedral but in the portals of the lower floor of the Audiencia (the building of the Municipal Council)."

1662.—"Birthday of the Vicereine. On the 25 of May, the Countess de Baños celebrated her birthday... All the ladies and women of the retinue were invited to the Palace richly adorned, and they attended the drama which was performed for them by the household servants of the Viceroys."—"Sunday, 11 of June, week following Corpus, the Viceroy had the play which was supposed to be performed as usual in the theater of the Cathedral cemetery staged in the late evening in the patio of the Palace, where the baptismal font is, so that the Vicereine and the servants might see it, since the Vicereine is pregnant."

Among other works of the seventeenth century, which belong to the second half and are largely lost, can be mentioned those of Juan Ortiz de Torres, Jerónimo Becerra, Antonio Medina Soler, Alfonso Ramírez de Vargas and Agustín Salazar y Torres. The first three wrote only *loas,* as did Ramírez de Vargas, who is, nevertheless, more outstanding because of his drama *The Greatest Triumph of Diana,* which was performed at the University. More substantial is the last of the group, of course. Salazar y Torres, the nephew of the Viceroy Torres y Rueda, was a Spaniard from Soria, where he was born on August 28, 1642. Brought to Mexico by his uncle at five years of age, he was educated in the schools and University here and wrote poetry precociously: the *Poetry Contest* of the literary University, published in Mexico City in 1654, contains several of his compositions. *Choose Your Enemy, The Olympic Games* and *Enchantment is Beauty and Fascination without Bewitchment* or *The Second Celestina* are his best-known plays which have been preserved in print. He did not succeed in finishing the last one, and in his place Juan de Vera Tasis completed it "by sovereign decree." He left Mexico in 1660, and died in Madrid in November, 1675. Spanish in all respects, he is justly not omitted from our histories of Mexican literature: "His friend Juan de Vera Tasis honored his memory by presenting in 1695, with the title of *Apollo's Cithar,* two volumes, one of poetry and another of plays... Among the works mentioned of this poet there are some that refer to matters in New Spain, such as the 'Description in Spanish Verse of the Arrival in Mexico City of the Viceroy Duke of Alburquerque,' the 'Mexican Transformations' and some others." Spain, furthermore, places him among the several successors to Lope de Vega.

Not without a prior motive, I request permission to quote again from the newspapers:

1675.—January. "Sunday the 27th, the Royal University of this Court celebrated a festival to the Immaculate Conception of Our Lady, the celebration lasted three days, and afterwards the students performed a play."—November. "Wednesday the 6th, the Viceroy's birthday was celebrated and there was a play at the Palace."

1677.—August. "Monday the 9th there was the festival with a sermon... and at the entrance there was a play by Cardinal Francisco Jiménez."

In the years 1678 and 1679 there were plays in the Palace to celebrate the birthdays of the Viceroy, and in the former year one was staged with the title *It Cannot Be.* Later on, those courtly performances continue to be carried out on analagous occasions and also on the birthdays of the Viceroy and the Prince (1684, 1688). However, the news of performances on religious occasions no longer appears. Granted that the stages erected by the municipal government existed previously, perhaps the farces of war known as *Conquests,* which were mentioned before and of which no example survives, were performed there with rudimentary equipment. Probably as a degeneration of this form, however, there continue to exist the spoken challenges between Moors and Christians, which at this time are still performed in some parts of the nation in conjunction with dances, as Francisco Monterde informs me. The limitation or disappearance of the earlier performances is due, apparently, to the restriction of the dramatic art to a more suitable theater located in the vicinity of the cemetery of the Royal Hospital for Illegitimates, which the Brothers of Saint Hippolytus ran for the benefit of the sick. Although the charter of the Hospital dates from 1553, the date on which the theater was first opened is not indicated. It was without question in the seventeenth century, and not at the beginning even though some say in 1673 — a date which is found in the record of an early inventory — for it had already been in existence for many years at that time. Judging by the excerpts from the newspapers which I have inserted, I believe that this first coliseum dates from the second half of the century, and perhaps from the second decade, an epoch in which the theater displays an orientation toward a strictly professional nature. An unclear note from the diary of Antonio de Robles says: "1675.—February, Monday the 4th. Today the company of actors went up to the Coliseum." The company was formed and well known prior to that date. It seems to have performed already in the Coliseum in 1673, and in it were Mateo de Jaramillo, author and director; Isabel Gertrudis; Josefa and Micaela Ortiz; Antonia de Toledo; Francisco de Castro; José Martínez; Antonio, Ventura and Bartolomé Gómez; Diego Jaramillo; Felipe de Viaja; Lorenzo Vargas and Juan de Saldaña, surely Spaniards, although nothing concrete is known to this effect.

My hypothesis being brought in this way to the point indicated I learned that, according to information belonging to Manuel Mañón, although the theater might have been built after 1553, the date on the charter of the Hospital, it was not built until 1671, which seems to be perfectly plausible.

Jaramillo seems to have been replaced in his position as playwright by a certain Ignacio Marqués, who in 1682 resigned. So as to continue the performances without a writer, the actors who formed the troupe met at the house of the presbyter Antonio Acosta, the administrator of the Royal Hospital on whom the responsibility for management of the theater fell, and agreed to seek the plays which were "most in fashion, and to accept without protest whatever role was assigned to them." Their names, which are preserved, were: Bernarda Pérez de Rivera, María F., Ana de Villegas, María Ortiz de Jaramillo, Mateo Jaramillo, Ignacia de Cárdenas, Juan de Dios, Antonio de Pinto, Diego de Sevilla, Juan Ferrete, Juan Ortiz de Torres — certainly the author of *loas* mentioned previously — and Antonio Ventura de Cerdán.

In the meantime, theatrical literature is less brilliant than ever. Francisco del Paso y Troncoso also translated into Spanish two anonymous autos written in Nahuatl, one in 1678 entitled *The Sacrifice of Isaac,* and another, *The Destruction of Jerusalem,* written in the handwriting of the late seventeenth century. The colloquy written in Nahuatl and translated by the same scholar, which was entitled *The Invention of the Cross by Saint Helen* and was published by the translator in a limited edition of fifty copies which are now unavailable, probably belonged to the same century.

Plays, *autos* and *loas* by Sor Juana Inés de la Cruz were also performed — the plays in the Palace theater — and, finally, the examples or models introduced at the end of the sixteenth century by Fray Juan de Torquemada continued to be performed. In the Hospital of Jesus Nazarene, Father Zappa recited a *nescuitile* (sic) in Nahuatl on January 17, 1690.

PAUSE

JUANA INÉS DE LA CRUZ was born at the granary at San Miguel Nepantla, Amecameca, on November 12, 1651, for the renewal of lyric poetry and the theater.

Like Juan Ruiz de Alarcón, she is a figure of particular singularity in her time, a perfect creature of letters, a child prodigy like Jacqueline Pascal at Port-Royal before her and, also like her, describable in the terms of Friedrich Nietzsche.

There exists between her and her century the same difference that exists between eyes which are open and eyes which are closed. Totally charming, she is the first florid product of a struggle of one hundred and thirty two years between totally different races in which victories are a tradition and defeats are assimilated. She is born with both resounding external power and an internal and silent strength. She reverberates in the claustral literature of that totally medieval period with a glimmer of anticipation, and what is to come can be perceived in her. Her voice, while extraordinary, is at the same time strange. A notorious example of order and mental clarity, she does not confuse her vocations but directs the rhythm of each one with lucid control and an eagerness for fecundity. Her monastic existence, which Ermilo Abreu Gómez correctly perceives to be purely ritualistic, is fecund. Her contact with the courtly world, which she witnesses for the first time and finds to be such a glittering phenomenon, is fecund. The communication which she establishes from her cell at San Jerónimo — by means of maps, texts, scientific instruments and music — with the thought of a world which is beginning to penetrate and to discover itself, is fecund.

Juana de Asbaje has little of the awesome literary woman; little or nothing of the irremediably common woman. There is in her a constant oscillation between wisdom and mischief, something which is always intact, spontaneous and fresh, surrounded by something which is always cultivated. She has limits; not of the type that can not be overcome, but of the kind that must be reached. She seems perfectly balanced to me, and full to the brim without a drop spilling over. She will not have a successor in the same way that Alarcón had none. It is difficult to be that way. The variations of her voice are not variances of value, but of scale. Pure and convincing in *villancicos, autos* and *loas,* it is pure, serious, simple and sweet in her love sonnets; pure and deliberate, although resonant, in the *redondillas* which were her principal guide through the world; it is pure and playful as it blends with the lilting dialects of Indians and Negros. Her voice, which in works of circumstance and praise is considered inferior, is in her quatrains pure, elegant, and polite; and if it is clear and sure in the theological prose, nothing of its purity nor its completeness is lost in them. Her voice is, in all genres, a phenomenon of purity, a lead instrument among all those of Spanish poetry from her times to the present. She is the light-handed mistress of form to such a degree that if she is ahead of her century in thought, in vision and feminine theories, her expression is not for one moment incomprehensible nor suspect, even though she may speak learnedly at times because her "Gongorism possessed something of mere literary virtuosity" and "was not a genuine and sincere manifestation of her mind, by nature crystalline and diaphanous."

The Marquis of Mancera and Fray Payo Enríquez de Rivera — among others wiser and more educated and without official motives — proclaim a sentiment which would not suffice were it only respect, because it is sympathy, not merely admiration, but esteem.

The biographers of Sor Juana — numerous inasmuch as they are biographers, and capable even if they are not illustrious — have busied themselves with brilliant expansiveness regarding the various facts of her life, and particularly with two: the reason which she had for becoming a nun, and the reason for her renunciation of literature and her abstention from study at a point at which — again extending our thanks to Abreu Gómez — she had surely reached Descartes. I could add little concerning the first matter, except that the concept of love is essential to Sor Juana and that a similar spirit could not avoid love — an enrichment — in her development.

VII.   Sor Juana Inés de la Cruz

Reproduced from the book *Mexican Painting and Painters,* by Robert H. Lamborn, Ph. D., Philadelphia, 1891.

Courtesy of the National Library of Mexico

Concerning the second matter, I believe that the thoughts and sentiments which led her to sign two protestations of faith in blood were not connected to, and inspired by, the letter of Sor Filotea alone. Her sensibility and her perception were as great as her curiosity and her equilibrium. How could she avoid exposure to the impersonal influence and atmosphere of the medievalism which ruled New Spain? Against her the Middle Ages took on human form in the Bishop of Puebla, Manuel Hernández de Santa Cruz, inappropriately named Sor Filotea, and in the Most Excellent Francisco Aguiar y Seijas, Archbishop of Mexico, the successor to, and opposite of, Fray Payo, whom Sor Juana so loved.

A harsh and ascetic preacher to whom plays were a vehicle of sin, Aguiar y Seijas, when he went on archiepiscopal pilgrimages throughout his diocese, preached, as José Lezamis said of himself, "with great acrimony against them," a genre which Sor Juana cultivated with viceregal applause and enthusiasm. Even during the festivals of the titular saints the Archbishop put the cross to the drama and traded tracts concerning alms ("Consolation of the Poor") for the sinful books of plays, which he had burned, catechizing for that purpose parishioners who were book dealers and readers.

I permit myself to think, contrary to distinguished opinions, that Sor Juana Inés' *villancicos* cannot be included in her dramatic work, and that her beautiful voyage through that genre is limited to her *Loa to the Conception*, her *autos The Martyr of the Sacrament, Saint Hermenegildo, The Scepter of Joseph* and *The Divine Narcissus* (the last from 1690, one of her last works), and her plays *The Obligations of a Home* and *Love is a Labyrinth*. All this in spite of the fact that her Christmas carols, because of their multiplicity of voices and their characteristics of a great instrument — an organ — are a good résumé of the talent of the tenth Muse.

Much has been said of the *culteranista* and Calderonian elements in the plays mentioned. I do not believe anything has been said concerning the similarity of plot that *The Obligations of a Home* shares with *The Woman Who was Discreet in Love,* by the inimitable Lope, whose expertise Sor Juana doubtlessly followed and admired. I insist that it was a similarity of points of departure and of dynamic phases only; form is personal in each, as is background, although both are equally discreet. More pleasing to me personally, furthermore, is the song sung in the drama of Sor Juana rather than the one in Lope's. At any rate, a plot of human fabrication, as soon as it is conceived and connected to the movement of reality by the characters, begins to be controlled by higher powers in both. Continuously there is manifested in both the intervention of an adversity and confusion which are wisely sought and clearly found by the dramatists. Also the Castaño of Sor Juana is very much more appealing to me than the Hernando of Lope de Vega, even though both servants are disguised as women. In addition, the axiomatic paradox is more brilliant in *The Obligations of a Home,* and the mischief more — dare I say mischievous? — and spontaneous. This general analogy may be satisfactorily explained by the practice imposed, in groups of "fifteen hundred" plays by the Spaniard.

The verse of Juana de Asbaje is limpid and full, compact and a little *conceptista,* "at the same time that it recalls, because of the noble, pure and sententious form of its concepts, Juan Ruiz de Alarcón y Mendoza, perhaps at times even surpassing it. We might almost say that it almost always does, for Sor Juana was more purely a poet than Alarcón. Her facility, her conversation, shine enchantingly in this play which Ezequiel A. Chávez claims is in all probability autobiographical.

The scholar Juan de Guevara, a cousin of Sor Juana Inés de la Cruz according to Francisco Fernández del Castillo, collaborated with her on the second act of *Love is a Labyrinth* (more a labyrinth than the one in Crete). Theseus, Ariadne and Phaedra participate in this Greek drama, and it can be considered as a theoretical treatise on the hero. "A hero to Sor Juana, as well as to Juan Ruiz de Alarcón y Mendoza, is he who, even when he has the most illustrious ancestry, gives himself credit for no more nobility than his own deeds warrant."

With regard to the *autos* of Sor Juana, in them the mystical and nationalistic tendency is similarly expressed. The former is characterized by a purity and such a classical sweetness that famous critics find in her verses the sixteenth century more than the seventeenth century, and they therefore recall the disciples of San Juan de la Cruz and Fray Luis de León (one such critic is Marcelino Menéndez y Pelayo). The latter is a constant sympathy for the

Indian, a protest against his social backwardness, against his lack of human worth for the plan of conquest in effect.

Before bringing this brief pause to a conclusion, it is fitting to mention the gift for dialogue apparent in all the dramatic works of Sor Juana. This is a theatrical gift if ever there was one. Not long ago, someone recalled the "fragrant visitation room of San Jerónimo" where "the melodious Sor Juana Inés de la Cruz had lively meetings every afternoon before vespers with the most substantial people of the city, ladies and gentlemen and even the viceroys themselves, who with their bejewelled following of courtiers went to be enthralled by the words of that nun who was 'superlative in every science.' "

Sor Juana died at four o'clock in the morning of April 17, 1695.

I terminate here this pause devoted to the only lyrical island whose earth may be kissed in the seventeenth century.

THE EIGHTEENTH CENTURY

THERE IS NO STAR in the Mexican theater in the course of the eighteenth century either. Following Navijo and Medina, who have already been mentioned, and the obscure performers who acted in the Society for Plays from 1597 on, from the time of the company of Mateo de Jaramillo at the theater of the Royal Hospital, the program announcements become numerous and uninteresting. I do not believe in the existence of a Burbage or a Molière, in spite of the leading man Diego Francisco de Asís or Diego de Asís Franco, to whom more space will be devoted later in this work. Nor does it seem to me that the theatrical assets of the theater are enriched with the brilliance of an Adrienne Lecouvreur, notwithstanding the "respected actress" Ana María de Castro, who will also figure later here.

Desolation continues in dramatic production. It is difficult to believe that numerous theatrical works were not written then. It is precisely in this century when the tendency toward nationalism, which reached its peak in 1810, begins to arise. Even when literary importation was still limited to products from Spain, many people of letters clung tenaciously to the idea of the evolution of the theater. Furthermore, the theater evolves by itself. The problems and customs of the country, more noticeable every day, were doubtlessly the backdrop for displays of all kinds, and even if no importation had been effected the writer who lacks ingenuity is a terribly sponta-neous plant, an individual who does not need original sin to come to life. Any man with an average education in the history of Mexico knew that the theater had been, together with firearms and horses, one of the most vigorous elements of persuasion employed by the conquerors, and how successfully it was utilized.

I believe that there were many writers of theatrical works in the seventeenth and eighteenth centuries; but I also believe that the precedent sown in the seventeenth century by Archbishop Aguiar y Seijas bore fruit, if not exactly abundantly, at least sufficiently to nourish ecclesiastical zeal. Nature does not tolerate idleness, and it has severe laws of reproduction which explain the always prevalent competition and the persistence of ugliness as well as beauty. Likewise, the successive religious authorities must have scrupulously maintained such a precedent. They were familiar with the persuasive dynamism of the theater and its direct impact on the multitudes, furthermore, more than the dramatists themselves. It is certain that they cut a goodly number of plays, in the form of printed works and manuscripts, to adorn the pious urns of censorship. The flowers of talent, it is maintained, are the best — personally I prefer red roses — and what a bouquet that must have been for the militant Church! This delicate gallantry was probably repeated with the most fastidious frequency during the course of the eighteenth century.

There is evidence that on Thursday, November 11, 1700, a stage was erected on the plaza of San Juan de Dios on which were performed, to celebrate the canonization of that saint, on the eleventh, *The Prodigious Prince,* and on the twelfth, *It Cannot Be,* works which are unknown today. It is also known that on Monday and Thursday of each week, at the theater of the Royal Hospital, free performances were given for the poor which were known by the name of *guanajas,* an expression which served to designate the outskirts of the city, in which performances were also given. These *guanajas* were commonplace already in 1707 and, apparently, "were given by arrangement with the Coliseum, as they were awarded in that year to Juan Gómez Medina, and in 1712 to Felipe Fernández de Santillana, because the Hospital no longer wanted to continue to manage them because of the absence of the first lady Antonia de Rivera, and because Gertrudis Cervantes had entered a convent and had decided to remain. In this year it seems that some reformation occurred, because the contractor took a position under the new arrangement in one of the articles which stated that the actors could not request fees in addition to their salaries."

The darkness remains: a play entitled *Roderick* (1708) and the first Mexican opera, *Parthenope* (1711) which still exists in printed form, both written by the presbyter Manuel Zumaya, were "both performed at the Viceregal Palace." Another presbyter, Cayetano Cabrera Quintero, wrote the plays *Hope Frustrated* and *The Rainbow of Salamanca*, about which the following is said:

"There is a play composed of Indian stories whose title in Spanish is *Hope Frustrated*. It consisted of several panegyrics in verse and in prose, "Dissertations in praise of Philosophy" and similar selections, which the erudite and curious preserve with consecutive pagination in a single volume at the time when the author (Cayetano de Cabrera y Quintero) had temporarily abandoned the teaching of Philosophy. Another play, whose title is *The Rainbow of Salamanca*, is taken from the story of Saint John of San Facundo. This play was performed at the Theater of Mexico City with great applause by the audience, and the Viceroy himself saw and praised it."

Francisco Soria had *William, Duke of Aquitaine, Mexican Magic* and *Genevieve* performed, which the chroniclers referred to as dramatic works. *The Mexican Portent* was composed by José Antonio Pérez y Fuentes, who is reputed to be the author of twenty *loas* in Nahuatl. Manuel Castro Salazar wrote a colloquy entitled *The Invention of the Cross*, which does not seem to me to be the one with a similar title translated by Francisco del Paso y Troncoso. *There is No Greater Evil Than Jealousy*, a play by Father Juan Arriola, and *The Trojan Woman*, a tragedy written by Father Agustín Castro, are both among works lost to time.

"1714.—On the occasion of the celebration of the Birth of the Child a partly public play was performed along with other festivities on January 22, in Taxco. Municipal Archive of Taxco."

It would be superfluous to speculate about the multiple limitations of the theater in the Colonial Period. It is only a matter of reverberations from Spain, where under Phillip II dramas are declared to be illegal, under the pretext that "they were illicit and it was a mortal sin to perform them"; where a theatrical regulation in 1615 prescribed three penalties, in ascending order, for violators: fines, exile and two years in the galleys; where, later, the plays of Lope de Vega are prohibited, and afterward the performances of all works that are not stories and lives of saints. It is certain that Phillip IV, whose residence at the Buen Retiro, includes a theater which is "the glory of the new palace," inaugurated under the direction of Pedro Calderón de la Barca, with whom Cósimo Lotti and Baccio del Bianco, who "invented marvelous sets and apparatus which served as a background for the characters of the dramatist" cooperate, rises up against all types of crime. But after Phillip died, in 1665, an order of the Queen causes theatrical performances to cease completely until her royal son Charles II, who was then four, is old enough to enjoy them.

It is not too much to assume, consequently, that the example of disciplines, fasts, and penitences which Spain imposed upon itself was followed, at least with equal rigor, in its dominions in the New World.

Josef and Eusebio Vela obtained the Coliseum in 1718 for three thousand pesos in the bidding for the concession. The latter "was a dramatic poet" — according to Beristáin — "if not equal to the Lopes and Calderóns, surely superior to the Montalbáns and Moretos in the decency of his jests." Furthermore, he considers him to be the most important dramatist of the eighteenth century, and it is possible, at least, to mention his works: *The Greatest of the Least, Saint Francis, The Asturian in The Indies; The Deceiver Deceived; Love Thy Neighbor; The Constancy of Spanish Women; Maddened by Insults, Calmed by Jealousy; Reaching the Heights of Happiness Through the Dangers of Love; Love Exceeds Art; If Love Exceeds Art Be Prudent in Neither; The Conquest of Mexico,* in three parts; *The Apostleship in the Indies; The Loss of Spain Because of a Woman,* and *The Love Most Prized between Treason and Prudence.* A Mexican, his works contain Mexican themes and purely national allusions, and such a prodigious or well received production cannot be attributed to anyone else in this century.

A play entitled *The Destruction and Burning of Jerusalem or Vindication of Christ* having been performed in the Coliseum on January 19, 1722 — which supposedly was performed in England with the title *The Miracles of Saint Catharine* —, it happened that between that night after the performance and the next morning the theater was destroyed by fire. About January 20, another play was announced surrounding the title of which — *Troy was Here* — all manner of superstitious symbols and fatalistic statements have revolved. In the place of the theater which burned another was erected, also of wood. But later another, which is designated as the third coliseum, was built in 1725 on land also belonging to the Royal Hospital and situated between the alley named Espíritu Santo and Azequia Street, and it was called the Old Coliseum. Let it be pointed out in passing that the modern Acequia Streets (J.O. de Domínguez District) did not yet exist at that time, when an actual cistern girded the Viceregal Palace. Neither the second nor the third Coliseums allegedly approached the "solidity and magnificence of the first."

For the years 1728 and 1729, the gazettes mention various performances staged in the Palace theater with no additional facts, as usual, concerning authors and actors.

To celebrate the canonization of Saint Luis Gonzaga and Saint Stanislas of Kostka, the Society of Jesus held solemn feasts which lasted from November 12 through 28, 1728, with four colloquies performed on the thirteenth of the month entitled: *The Triumphs of Heaven, Virtue Crowned, The Harmony of the Sciences* and *The Obligations of Paradise.* On September 19, of the same year, the birthday of the King provided an illustrious occasion for several celebrations about which there is an account of the performance in the Palace theater of the play *Even Jealousy of Nothing is Deadly.* The year 1729 offers several performances. In the festivals that were celebrated by the religious Carmelites from January 15 to 24, to solemnify the canonization of Saint John of the Cross, plays were performed, and on September 19, the new birthday of His Majesty, there was produced in the Palace the play entitled *Love Exceeds the Art and Inventions of Archimedes,* the first part of whose title is reminiscent of a work by Eusebio Vela to such a degree that it can be supposed that it is a matter of two different plays only because of the description.

The first outstanding theatrical performers known in Mexico played in the third Coliseum, notwithstanding its "poor construction." Among them was the Spanish actor Esteban Vela, who managed the Coliseum beginning in 1731, who must be considered as one of the most prominent. It is told about him that he performed very well on the stage. So well, in fact, that after the five year period elapsed during which he had rented the theater, he succeeded in obtaining the renewal of the contract for nine years, thanks to the support of the canon Luis Antonio de Torres, administrator of the Royal Hospital for Illegitimates, even though

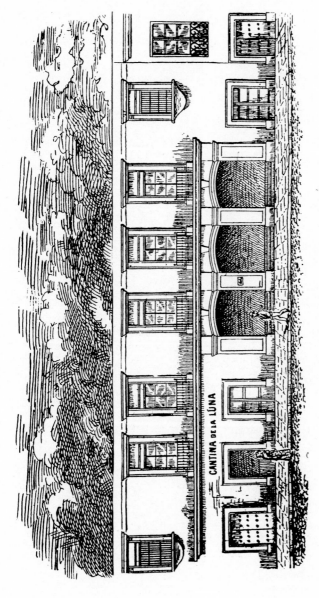

VIII.   The New Coliseum (1753)

Reproduced from the book *México
Viejo*, by Luis González Obregón

*Courtesy of the National Library of
Mexico*

there was competition, because the latter judged that Vela would bring advantages to the theater since his skill and "the just acclaim that he had acquired for himself" were so well known. The members of the troupe of Esteban Vela were: Felipe Sánchez, Nicolás Campos, Alejandro Monzón, Clemente Figueredo, and Diego Francisco de Asís. Vela having died during the course of the nine years during which his contract had been renewed, the actress Ana María de Castro asked for, and obtained, the direction of the theater in spite of the lawsuit brought against her by Vela's widow, who sought control in her own behalf.

Ana María de Castro had already acquired by that time a solid reputation and was, as reports have it, enthusiastically applauded and admired. Her luxurious wardrobe is spoken of with grandiose adjectives, and Francisco de Chávarri praised her, after consultation with the Viceroy, in these terms: "Her energy in performing, her understanding of the verse, her elocution, rhetoric, and the vividness of her actions, the sweetness and harmony of her voice when she sings, are all acclaimed by the public."

Although she was the mistress and tyrant of public taste, and the possessor of a complete troupe in which she and Diego Francisco de Asís were the principal figures, Ana María de Castro suddenly retired from the theater, having been converted by the sermons of Father Matías Conchoso, according to Beristáin. This must have happened in 1742, the same year in which Josef Cárdenas, then administrator of the Royal Hospital, honorary custodian of the Royal Tribunal of Accounts and noted supporter of the theater, obtained royal permission to place under contract "some talent for this Coliseum." This importation seems to have elevated the activity of the theater in Mexico to a high degree. In 1742 and 1743, Cárdenas employed Josef Ordóñez, Isabel Gamarra — his wife — and his two daughters Vicenta and Josefa, of which the last was later "a lady of the theater of great reputation and who married the famous Panseco." The other persons employed were: Juan Gregorio Panseco, "a native of Milan, musician of the naval battalions and expert in the playing of the violin, the double bass, and the German flute"; Josef Pisoni "of the Duchy of Milan, expert at the violin, French horn, and dancemaster"; Jean Baptiste Arestin, "A Frenchman expert at the violin and double bass"; Gaspar and Andrés Espinosa, "players of the French horn, German flute, violin and oboe"; Benito Andrés Preibus, "of the port of Santa María, who had the same talent as the two aforementioned"; Francisco Rueda, "excellent in violin and French horn," and his wife Petronila Ordóñez, "a famous actress and excellent singer, who accompanied herself marvelously with violin and guitar," both of the theater of Barcelona, and, finally, the "famous musician-composer Ignacio Jerusalem, a native of the city of Leche in the Kingdom of Naples, a Kapellmeister who later was at this Holy Cathedral where, during the matins of his composition played here on Holy Thursday of the year 1753, apart from the enormous crowd in attendance to hear them, their Excellencies the Viceroy and his wife were present."

In addition, the practice of the dramatic art had become widespread in the entire country, and in the towns and cities of lesser importance the drama attached itself, as in the capital, to the diverse festivals celebrated on religious or court occasions. The statement which I transcribe subsequently, and for which I am in debt to Francisco Monterde, confirms this:

"...The Parade through the City having ended, the Royal Standard was placed in a very proper and public place underneath a Canopy on a pillow of Velvet, and / at night there were many festival lights, with several sallies into the countryside; with different pealings of the bells in our Church which was replete with decorations; which was followed by a very resplendent triumphal Carriage with the coat-of-arms of Spain, Scepter and Imperial / crown; and in that Carriage was a character who performed in three sep / arate parts a very learned *Loa* in praise of our King and Lord Ferdi / nand the Sixth; with Much acclaim by the People, with many Shouts and Hurrahs for / our King and Lord, Ferdinand the Sixth; all of which ended tonight (January 24, 1748).—On the 26th, in the morning and afternoon, there was for the enjoyment of the City, and to Further Solemnize / the Oath of Office of our King and Lord, a Bullfight, and the Twenty-seventh Day; there was a very good / Play, which terminated the festivals." (Statement of Fray Lorenzo Antt° Estremera about the Solemn Oath of Ferdinand VI. Santa Fe, New Mexico.)

The Coliseum was in such a deplorable state in the year 1749 — the same year in which a high decree forbade the wonderful side balconies and separated the galleries of men and women — that after an inspection by the authorities its performances were suspended. The concessionaire of the theater at that time was the leading lady Josefa Ordóñez, who after making certain official contacts succeeded in arranging the approval by the building contractor Felipe Cortés of the proposal of the Master architect Lorenzo Rodríguez, who committed himself to repairing the Coliseum in three weeks for a cost of 1500 pesos in order to make it usable for ten or twelve additional years. The work seems to have been carried out and to have been inspected to the satisfaction of the contractor.

The leading man, Diego de Asís Franco, died at age forty-five on January 27, 1753. He was a native of San Angel, and in spite of his profession was a person of great virtue, judging by the fact that he was given a Christian burial in the church of the Convent of San Bernardo. He is mentioned as "very practiced and skilled in his art, and is sorely missed in his troupe because there is no one to equal him in this exercise."

There is another great event in this same year of 1753, and it is the inauguration, on December 25, of a new coliseum built of stone which existed until our times with the name Teatro Principal; it continued to exist until it was destroyed by fire during the night of March 1, 1931. This enterprise was carried out by Josef Cárdenas, the true precursor of our theatrical promoters, in spite of the "unpleasantness, fatigue and worries" which the Coliseum reportedly caused him. Of a poorly constructed oviform shape, it looked more like a horseshoe when finished, the new theater was built by Eduardo Herrera and Manuel Alvarez at the expense of the Hospital on lands occupied by the houses of a certain Josef Gorráez y Luyando. Here a circumstantial play, *It is Better than It Was,* was performed with the Viceroys presiding over the large audience in attendance that night.

The death of King Ferdinand VI in 1759, and that of the Viceroy Marquis de las Amarillas, the scandalous expulsion of the Jesuits, the threat of war between the Spanish and English and, in general, any event of whatever age or social position, shackled the performances of our theater, which could not attain an exclusively popular and professional life because of its fatal dependence upon governments and medieval practices in Mexico. However, several Viceroys — Antonio de Bucareli y Ursúa, second

Count of Revilla Gigedo among others — protected theatrical performances. The first formal regulation, which consisted of twenty-five articles edited by Basilio de Villarrasa Venegas, modified by the attorney-general and approved by Antonio María de Bucareli, was imposed on the theater in 1779.

The manuscript of *Adoration of the Magi,* written anonymously and translated from the Nahuatl by Francisco del Paso y Troncoso, dates from 1760, although it was apparently written in the second half of the sixteenth century.

Two free performances of *Meet Disdain with Disdain* and *The Enemy of Women* were given on June 21 and 22, 1785, on the occasion of the celebration of the arrival in the capital of the Viceroy Count de Gálvez. In addition, court-day, bull-baiting, open house in an anteroom of the Palace, and a nocturnal performance of the play *The Innocent Found Guilty,* figured among the festivities given in honor of the Viceroy's son, Miguel Gálvez, on September 29, 1785. The index of the Municipal Archive of Veracruz shows that in that same year a document by "Joseph Sánchez... requesting a license for the performance of plays under the terms stated..." was presented.

It seems that between 1775 and 1786 the works of Calderón de la Barca (*Life is a Dream*), performed together with farces, musical interludes, dances, operas and plays, kept the theater going, however slowly, in spite of the thousand handicaps of different types in cause and effect such as theatrical ordinances which, under the viceroyalty of Count de Gálvez, prescribed the installation of a border of one tercet in height on the front edge of the stage so that the actresses' feet could not be seen. In its turn, the puppet theater had existed for a long time, and was regulated officially in the year 1786.

The appearance of the *Mexican Gazette,* in 1784, did not contribute to our being overwhelmed with detailed news about the theater, even when it mentioned the plays performed at the Palace and announced those at the Coliseum, for it refrained discreetly from mentioning the authors and actors, a custom which remains with us for some time, at least insofar as the former are concerned.

1787.—"Document of the directors of the Corporation of the Coliseum to the City Council of Veracruz requesting a license to begin performances at the cockfighting ring while the Coliseum is shut down temporarily.—Index of the Municipal Archive of Veracruz."

In 1790 a gentleman named Ramón Blascio petitioned for the theatrical concession in Mexico City for a five year period. His request was denied, even though Blascio went on to become the sponsor of the future importers of European theatrical material, of translators and arrangers, whose present day abundance has all the characteristics of an illness. All of this is taken, at any rate, from his petition to the Viceroy, in which he speaks of doing everything in European fashion including performances and dances, and of importing works by Calderón, Moreto, and of the writers considered to be the best.

My theory that there were many theatrical works written and few performed becomes more acceptable if it is kept in mind that dramatic performances in Mexico justified the appointment of a censor, a post held by Father Ramón Fernández del Rincón (1790).

It seems that in the year 1793 he exercised his fatal influence also over Mexican authors, since it was already official policy for entrepreneurs, in order not to pay royalties, to reject their works while pretending that Spanish ones, for which they had to pay nothing, were superior.

1798.—"Theatrical season formulated in Veracruz by Leandro Manero. Index of the Municipal Archive of Veracruz."

Many of the *loas,* anonymous or signed, which were usually performed on the occasion of the arrivals of the viceroys, together with numerous discourses which were recited by professional actors in the guise of exegeses of the statues which decorated the portals prepared for such occasions, have been preserved up to the present time. The majority of the ones in existence belong to the eighteenth century.

Pointing out in passing the appearance of a new genre related to literature, bibliography, we can throw away the key to the eighteenth century which, because of the absence of nobler merits, can claim to have defined with greater or lesser exactitude the general future of the theater in Mexico: foreign actors, foreign works, systematic opposition of enterprises to national authors, insistence on giving the Mexican public a false theatrical education which still burdens it. And there are other equally curious things which disguise, with marvelous trappings, the fact that there are dramatists in Mexico.

THE NINETEENTH CENTURY

Obverse

THE MIDDLE AGES are about to end in Mexico. The last third of the previous century has seen events with a new impetus arise, and previously unknown sentiments have become airborne in several European countries. This infant which is being born has been taking shape for centuries in the ether, and what is erupting in the world is the perfect culmination of a culture within the individual. New conquerors, the new thoughts likewise feel the cosmic attraction of America and also discover it.

Because of the terribly lenient censorship of the Holy Office, the social doctrine of Voltaire and the natural theory of Rousseau flourish in Mexico. The uneasiness of the entire world has made itself felt here, moreover, since the second half of the eighteenth century. Experimentation in the sciences, the muted scholastic war in philosophy, brash neoclassical experiments in literature, coincided with an early period of plenitude in the plastic arts and in architecture. But here it is not the autoctonous dynasties, as in other countries — from Egypt onward —, that have shaped their power in the work of the architects in order to fall back into the error of Nietzsche. When the monarchies of the pyramids became extinct, when their descendants were subjected and transformed, other men worked at the creation of a strange power whose tenets are suspect now to the new race which has gradually been formed, and whose own land is both wellspring and mother of that power. And the will of that race slowly makes its way toward the light in order to proceed from the light to possession of it. It reaches the need for total expression. Will it use the theater to obtain it? The hope is brief — for that reason it is so durable — and the plural realities of Mexican life will still prefer other routes.

From 1784 on, with the appearance of the *Mexican Gazette* which has been previously mentioned, journalism begins its work of deception in the country in the most serious way. Neoclassicism, a train with lyrical landscape decals on its windows beside which unexpected shepherds pasture false flocks while applying names of intangible and mysterious grace to each other, begins to run on its rails.

The Coliseum continues to operate. The theater may not be alive, but nowhere does it die. In spite of the fact that there is not a wealth of material available between 1800 and 1805, there can be ascertained from the witty and exaggerated *Gazette* of Manuel Antonio Valdés that on February 4, 1800, the city of Durango distinguishes itself with the inauguration of a coliseum which features the performance of the first part of *Andromaque*. Elsewhere, the arrivals of viceroys in the capital (Félix Berenguer de Marquina on April 28, 1800) and the anniversary celebrations of the monarchs (the birthday of the Prince of Asturias on October 14, 1800) continue to be heralded with theatrical performances which are staged, almost without exception by now, at the Coliseum. Slowly, but surely, a professional nucleus is being formed in the theater. The carefully observed custom of dedicating performances to the reigning authority — whoever it may have been, let it be said in all fairness — reaches at about this time a degree of stability which will preserve it for many years.

The Holy Office, which will perish for lack of evolution, justifies its existence by means of unvarying activity. In a royal decree of His Majesty on February 16, 1801, numerous works are condemned, of which I shall mention the dramas, and are prohibited *in totum*:

"17.—*The Debt Repaid,* by Lope de Vega Carpio. The performance and reading of this play are prohibited because it is deemed prejudicial to good taste." 22.—"The heroic drama in three acts entitled *The Siege of Calés,* by Luciano Francisco Comella, is prohibited from being read or performed because it contains instruction in suicide and fanaticism." 23.—"*The Unfortunate Lovers or the Count of Cominge*: a drama in three acts written in French by M. D. Arnaud, with translation into Spanish by Manuel Bellosartes, is prohibited from being performed and read because it is scandalous to the faithful and is in violation of rule seven of the Index of Forbidden Books." 24.—"*A Pitiful Tragedy,* which presents the passion and death of Christ Our Lord composed by a religious member of the Congregation of the Hospital of Vich, is prohibited from being performed or read because in some acts it is not sufficiently accurate and in conformity with the story that it recounts and with the pure and common doctrine of the Holy Fathers, and because the performance of this type of drama has been forbidden in numerous Royal Decrees." 28.—"*The Infancy of Jesus Christ*: a dramatic poem: a quarto volume printed in Málaga in the Office of the Heirs of Francisco Martínez de Aguilar: its author Gaspar Fernández de Avila: because it is, in spite of the good intentions and commendable zeal of its author, a derisive and abusive work in matters concerning the Holy Scripture, and is in formal violation of the Decree of the Council of Trent, section four, last paragraph." 30.—"*What Happens in a Nun's Turnstyle*: a drama printed in Córdova, at the Colegio de la Asunción, with no author's name or year of imprint: because it is in violation of the seventh and eleventh rules of the Index of Forbidden Books, and because it ridicules the Religious vocation and persons devoted to the Lord."

Later — June 30, 1804 — another edict prohibits "even for those who have a dispensation," "The chef d'œuvres" (sic) by Pierre and Thomas Corneille, "a new expanded edition of the Notes and Commentaries of M. de Voltaire," noting particularly that "the prohibition does not include the plays contained in this collection, and concerns only the notes of Volter (sic), because they contain impious, sacrilegious and heretical doctrines, and all the works of this Heresiarch are prohibited even for those with a dispensation."

The state of dramatic literature is, then, as grave as can be imagined. Apparently there are no Mexican works even among those prohibited by the Holy Tribunal of the Faith.

With the appearance of *El Diario de México,* on October 1, 1805, things change somewhat; the notion of news is refined among editors, and the public spectacles of the city are spoken of in greater detail. As concerned as I am about authors, I shall not speak yet about the actors. In *El Diario* of December 10, 1805, a contest is announced in which a prize of twenty-five pesos will be paid for the best *sainete* presented before February 15. The standard for the plays submitted, "or for their length, should be worked out on the basis of those of Ramón de la Cruz. Apart from the dramatic rules, humor which may offend modesty and decorum must be avoided." After misinterpretations of those rules, which cause the submission of a composition which "has merit but is not a *sainete*," a play entitled *Prudence Redeems the Greatest Libertinism* is received, which is reviewed unfavorably from the beginning in *El Diario* by Francisco Marniau y Torquemada, with whom the two other judges appear to agree. Then on June 20, 1806: "The examination of the *sainetes* entitled *White by Necessity* and *Unjustified Complaints,* which are the only entries, having been read separately by three judges, it was unanimously agreed that the prize should be given to the former." The author turned out to be a certain Antonio Santa Ana, ninety years of age, who was a captain in the Provincial Militia Company of Negroes of Veracruz. "The giver of the prize (Juan Bautista Arizpe) is attending to the appropriate requirements so that the play may be performed in the theater of this Court, and to the details of printing." The additional offer of doing everything possible to see that the other *sainete, Unjustified Complaints,* was performed was made together with the announcement of a new contest: "Twenty-five pesos to the author of the best *sainete* which is composed and presented before November 4. Consult the restrictions described in issue number 71, and be aware of the fact that in order to win the prize it will not be sufficient that the play be the best of those presented, but that it be worthy in and of itself... Another prize of one hundred pesos is offered under similar conditions to whoever composes and presents the best play before June 13 of next year, 1807."

In order to give an idea of what theatrical performances were like at the time, together with the announcements made by *El Diario,* the following form the Wednesday, February 12, 1806 edition will suffice:

"*His Son Recognized,* a play in two acts with Luciano Cortés playing the old man; *The Winsome Paca, sainete*: a song by María Josefa Cárdenas, and another sung in four parts; the small dance group of the little Negresses, and the large troupe of Adelayde de Güesclin." (Sic.)

It is now necessary to salute the Unknown Subscriber who, on March 11, 1806, concerning himself with the public entertainment of the city, said: "The principal one (diversion or spectacle) is the drama. Its sets are good: the actors are not bad: among them are some, ay (ay!) who might star in Madrid itself, and in Naples: the theater is comfortable: in it, orderliness is maintained by the vigilance of the constables. It only remains for us to ask why the sensible part of the audience joins in the applause for some *entremeses* which are staged only to placate the vile rabble?"

Ordinary and extraordinary performances, widely acclaimed variety shows with a gamut of numbers, include, in the year 1806, dramas, *sainetes,* dance steps (like the *Zanganito,* for four people), Polish dances, *boleras, bambas, sonecitos* (one was about a little reed), *zorzicos,* and popular songs (one is about a small child, in four-four time). Among the numerous plays and *sainetes* announced in *El Diario,* I select from those which for various reasons deserve the greatest attention: "*The Café,* never performed in this Theater, by the famous Moratín" (April 11); *The Duke of Pentiebre or The Othelloess*: "a work of recognized merit by the famous Arellano"; *The Captive Galley Slave,* "with Fernando Gávila in the leading role, and with Luciano Cortés as the *gracioso*; *The False Nuncio from Portugal,* a Mexican work presented by a subscriber to *El Diario* with the award for being "the worst of our awful plays," which as prohibited in *totum* by the Holy Tribunal of the Faith in 1809, although certainly not because of its quality; *Among Fools Gambling Runs Rampant and All Were Cheaters* is one of those which survive; "the play entitled *Othello*"; the *zarzuela Isabela*; *The Weaver of Segovia,* by Juan Ruiz de Alarcón; *Napoleon Bonaparte at Adige Pass and the Battle of Arcole,* "a new heroic, original drama written by a member of this theater"; *Master Vidriera*; *The Rising Sun of Spain and Toledano Moisés,* "with Dolores Tapia, alias The Star, playing the role of the leading lady"; *Emilia*; *Themistocles*; *White by Necessity,* performed in a variety show on July 9; *Christopher Columbus*; *Bonaparte in Egypt and The Taking of Cairo*; *The Stone Guest*; *Cortés in Tabasco*; *Paul and Virginia,* "a pastoral drama"; *The Prodigious Prince,* which judging by the title, could come from 1700; *The Conquest of Mexico,* staged on August 13, and followed by, at least up until that time, the traditional custom; *The Marriage of Indians*; the tragedy *La*

Shore; *The Sensitive Negro,* certainly a Mexican melodrama which, because it became very popular, was prohibited *in totum* by the Holy Tribunal on August 5, 1809 because it encouraged the insurrection of slaves against their masters and for which "The Mexican Thinker" would later write a second part; *The Pettifogger* and *The Mexican Woman in England,* works which are to all appearances Mexican; the two act tragedy *Othello*; *The Magician of Salerno*; *The Ring of Giges,* and *Bonaparte.* The age that several of these plays have attained is more than a century. From this year on (December 4), the Italian opera comes to Mexico with *The Barber of Seville* of Paisello. There is one dreadful note: the periods between acts are replete with Mexican songs.

The edicts concerning books continue to thunder forth: in 1807 there was the prohibition *in totum* of the "play *The Spanish Phoenix, The Martyr Saint Lorenzo,* Francisco Lozano, printed in Madrid in 1743, because it is scandalous and sacrilegious."

The previously mentioned drama contest yields no great productions. Only two plays are received, *Mamola* and *Florinda,* and nothing more is known about them. Furthermore the notices of performances which appeared in *El Diario* with regularity disappear and are seen only sporadically. In September, 1807, *One Madman Makes a Hundred,* by Rosa Gálvez is mentioned, and in October the printing firm of Arizpe announces, in an advertisement, the sale for four *reales* of *The Hidalgo in Medellín,* "a *sainete* which received the second prize, with an instructive prologue." Its author was a certain Juan Policarpo from Veracruz, and in this contest the first prize was won by *The Miserable Deceived One or The Maiden of the Half Almond,* written by Francisco Escolano y Obregón, which was performed on July 18, 1807. There is also the mention of three small plays entitled *The Death of The Chicken and Its Owner, The Hoax of the Small Tamales* and *Fasting in Order to Eat,* which Ramón Quintana mentions in a critical article without praising them a great deal. A performance in Guadalajara on December 12, 1807, includes the colloquy *The Appearances of Our Lady of Guadalupe* by the scholar José Beltrán, and among the foreign works appears *The Maidens' Consent* by Moratín (1808).

The contest for a national tragedy which is announced by *La Gaceta* and *El Diario* in March, 1808, requiring themes of Mexican extraction for the best use "of the antiquities of this hemisphere, which are unknown to Europeans," produces no results. A work which was not performed and is lost to us was the only flower plucked for it, *Xochitl*. The works are always lost; a large part of those cited together with the colloquies — which after 1815 will change their names, for the most part, to that of *pastorelas* — performed in theaters, *corrales* and family homes and whose performance Archbishop Lizana prohibits in December 1808.

Nevertheless, "Mexican authors did not remain totally alien to dramatic activity. Ochoa, Guridi y Alcocer, Barquera — among the best known — wrote for the stage; even if we only know the names of their works because they were never published." The Mexican theater, in general, is not published, and this is probably the reason for all the defects that it has had. A young man who does not travel never becomes famous; a woman who never goes out into the street feels no obligation to dress up.

Meanwhile, in general, the priests of the small towns of the country had performed, by and for their faithful, colloquies and *autos* with no other merit than tradition; a priest translated and staged works by Racine and Molière. Apparently a young woman named Josefa Quintana was in charge of playing the leading roles. The priest directed the works by himself, explaining them in detail to the actors, and among them he preferred, and had performed several times, *Le Tartuffe*. These diversions, which were extraordinary for the times, took place in the town of San Felipe de los Herreros or Torresmochas, Guanajuato, a few years before the War of Independence, that priest's name was Miguel Hidalgo y Costilla.

Three extracts from the Index of the Municipal Archive of Veracruz show that in 1805 Pedro García Urrego, Mariano Aguirre and Gertrudis Solís presented requests for the leasing of that coliseum; that in 1810 Antonio Rodríguez petitioned for the same reason stating, in addition, another request that the performance of a play for theatergoers be permitted, and that in 1812 the land where the coliseum was situated was purchased form the Fathers of Saint Augustine.

Moreover, a growing agitation concentrates all activities on two essential points. If in 1806 the praises of Napoleon were sung in adjectives in the very columns of *El Diario,* in 1808 he is slandered in them because of his war against Spain; traitors are burned who represent Joseph Bonaparte together with the "bottles" of the affair, and news from Spain is awaited with great anxiety. Ferdinand VII lives his hour as an idol in the mind of the colonial masses. Afterwards, naturally, it will be the struggle for independence which will command attention.

One can walk with ease through the desert which extends to 1821. There is not even a little wild grass, because of the lack of a theatrical meadow, where one could devote oneself to rest and contemplation. Only the absolute absence of great national actors explains why the insurgents have not utilized the theater in the new catechization of the people — where is there a Talma? — as the Russians would do a century later with their theatrical tyrants — Mayerhold, Ewreinoff — and their theater for the masses. No appeal is made to the rapidity of the means of persuasion for rapid education in a country with few who can read. To the contrary, it is a new literary generation — the pamphleteers — which tries to carry out such an undertaking. A curious thing occurs: in the pamphlets, on the other hand, frequent use is made of dialogue, and the orators join the political writers and pamphleteers. But none of these theatrical derivatives leads us to the theater. The theater falls after that under the role of two opposite definitions which will damage it for a long time; on occasion it will not be thought of as a literary genre at all; at other times it seems to be regarded as an exclusively literary genre. Furthermore, at that time lyric poetry is in vogue in literature. The violent state of action in the country tolerates theatrical performances, however, and probably is once more the vehicle for propaganda for realistic government. At least there are reports that it receives a degree of protection from the viceregal hand of Félix Calleja, who can be presumed to have been interested in it in 1813. In this same year, besides dramatic works, the operas *Clara and Adolfo, The Wooden Clock, The Little Sailor,* and *A Bit of Mischief* are performed, the latter having apparently met with great success. The Mexican opera, mentioned at the beginning of the previous century by the presbyter Zumaya as has been indicated, begins to tempt writers, Manuel de Arenzana, kapellmeister of the Cathedral of Puebla, was apparently "the second author of opera and the first in bringing to the stage of a public theater a work of such a type, for in the season, or "cosmic year" as it was called, from 1806 to 1807, on November

25, 1806 his opera in two acts *The Foreigner* was sung in the theater of the New Coliseum."

Criticism, which would have had so much influence on the theater if it had existed, is practiced by some subscribers to *El Diario,* among others a certain D. J. D., from whom the performance of the play *The Most Prodigious Negro* (1813) elicits bitter complaints and seems to him comparable in poor quality to the works *Genoveva, The Hidden Man and The Disguised Woman* and — poor Lope! — *The Girl with The Pitcher,* which "unfortunately have been performed lately."

Although the puppet theater seems to have been exploited beginning with the previous century, as was indicated, the historian Rangel points out the play *The Counterfeit Painter* and the *sainete Cafés and Inns* as the first works performed with puppets at a place named Palenque de Gallos (1814). A third opera — a comic one — is staged toward the end of 1816: *The Twins or The Uncle and Aunt Scorned*; perhaps it is related to the inevitable Menecmes, or to their teratological equivalent by Shakespeare; the libretto is by Ramón Roca, whose pen name is Marón Dáurico, and the music is by Manuel Corral, both Spaniards living in Mexico.

Neither the "Plan of the Three Guarantees" nor the achievement of independence had yet sounded when the bells of the nation ring to a tumultuous nationalism which lays siege to and conquers lyric poetry with almost mythological abandon which, after using the theater as a shelter, takes refuge in the novel, an even less accessible genre. Why? Probably because the theater is the final and perfect expression of all races; certainly because theatrical interpreters have not inspired any enthusiasm in men sufficiently unconcerned to write; but certainly also because no one knows with any clarity what the theater really is.

Anastasio María de Ochoa y Acuña arranges *Eugénie,* by Beaumarchais, writes two plays which take the wrong road, that is to say which are lost, and a tragedy, *Don Alfonso,* which is worse but is the only one of theatrical substance which is performed. José Agustín de Castro, the author of sacred poetry, *autos* and *loas* (*The Coming of the Holy Spirit, The Resurrection of Jesus Christ,* etc.) produces two *sainetes* with completely nationalistic titles: *The Cobblers* and *The Charro.* He has the merit of being the first in his century to introduce types, customs and popular language to the stage. Francisco Ortega stages *Mexico Freed* in 1821, probably a patriotic work, writes other unpublished plays, and translates into Spanish *Rosmunda* by Alfieri. José María Villaseñor y Cervantes composes *The Glory of the Nation Through Its King and Its Union,* and Juan Wenceslao Barquera leaves — where is not known — the manuscripts of three plays. The year 1823 salutes the semi-serious opera *Adela or the Constancy of Widows* by the scholar José María Moreno, a Mexican, and the tragedy of Martínez de la Rosa, entitled *The Widow of Padilla,* which is presented in April. *The Recluse,* an opera composed in Mexico by Esteban Cristiani, is performed in 1824, and between 1821 and 1824 *Pelayo,* by Quintana, is among the works produced. On October 15, still in 1824, the circumstantial tragedy *Regulus or Patriotism Triumphant* is produced on the occasion of president Guadalupe Victoria's coming to power.

Of relative importance in the theater, because of his pamphlets containing dialogues, José Joaquín Fernández de Lizardi devotes some attention to it nevertheless. He is a modern man, an adjective which should be understood in the sense of his having lived in his time; he believes in journalism, and is a believer in, and creator of, the novel in Mexico. I do not understand, however, why he did not direct his moralizing toward the theater; perhaps he lacked sufficient time, as generally occurs with all Mexican writers. The melodrama *The Sensitive Negro,* which will be remembered as having been performed with popular acclaim and having been prohibited in the first decade of the nineteenth century, has a second part written by Fernández de Lizardi in 1825. He is the author also of the *Marian Auto to Commemorate the Miraculous Appearance of Our Mother and Lady of Guadalupe,* of the *pastorela* entitled *The Happiest Night,* and it is said that he left unpublished *The Tragedy of Father Arenas,* in four acts in verse, and *The Unipersonal of don Agustín de Iturbide,* in eleven syllable verse with a name which was given to monologues at that time. In honor of the immemorial ill will of publisher toward writers it is not inappropriate to point out in passing that the publishers of *The Happiest Night* conferred this same title on another *pastorela* also published by them (*The Rewards of Innocence* by Ignacio Fernández Villa) which was only distributed for that reason, because they offered nothing in exchange for a Lizardi.

IX. Manuel Eduardo de Gorostiza
(Above left)

> Reproduced from the edition of
> his works by V. Agüeros

X. Ignacio Rodrigues Galván
(Above right)

> Reproduced from *El Museo Me-*
> *xicano*
>
> *Courtesy of the National Library*
> *of Mexico*

XI. José Rosas Moreno
(Below left)

> *Courtesy of Luis González Obre-*
> *gón*

XII. José Peón y Contreras
(Below right)

> Reproduced from the edition of
> his works by V. Agüeros in Me-
> xico City in 1896
>
> *Courtesy of Mrs. Isolina Varona,*
> *widow of Peón del Valle*

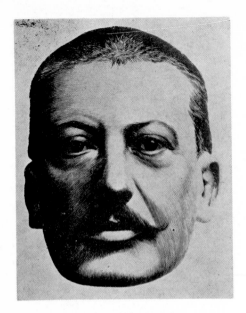

XIII. Manuel José Othón
(Mask by R. Durand) *(Above left)*
Courtesy of Jesús Zavala

XIV. Old Theatrical Poster
(Above right)
Courtesy of Manuel Villa Gordoa

XV. The Gran Teatro Nacional (1844) *(Below left)*
Courtesy of Miss Georgia Siverling

XVI. Angela Peralta *(Below right)*
Courtesy of Manuel Villa Gordoa

It is generally agreed that it is necessary to reach the works of Manuel Eduardo de Gorostiza in order to set foot on theatrical *terra firma* in the first third of this century. However strange it may seem, it is that way. Gorostiza is an honored guest in the Mexican theater. None of his plays is about Mexico — with the exception of the Negro in *Bread and Onions with You* — and, nevertheless, they are the ones which bring dignity and a decided modernity to the Mexican theater, even though Gorostiza's lead is not followed subsequently. His works have two perfectly distinctive points of balance: an equilibrium of language, which is as pure as is possible, and which does not age because the ribbons of the "newly coined" phrases which find favor in his era and are forgotten before they die do not spoil or discolor it, and an equilibrium of ideological clarity. Gorostiza knows the French theater, its espousal of the three unities and its panache of clarity. He introduces in his theater all that he can of the former without disguising it, and furthermore, since he does it from a higher plane, his personality suffers, consequently, no diminution of any sort. He thus constitutes another figure of elevation and solitude in the theater even though he writes classical plays like Moratín and Bretón de los Herreros.

Contemporary history having been converted in turn into a center for tourism for the loftiest Mexican writers, the theater continues to be subjected to ills associated with infancy. Until that time no ulterior tendencies or intentions have allied themselves with it. It lacks uniformity and harmony in its elaboration because it lacks a well elaborated school, and it has only been maintained by servants without initiative and tyrants. It is then that the young country leaps from the Middle Ages to Romanticism employing French and Byronian spurs for lyric poetry and Spanish spurs for the theater. In 1838 (September 27), Ignacio Rodríguez Galván produces *Muñoz, Inspector of Mexico.*

His bitter childhood — so often recounted and commented upon in the style of his times —, his juvenile and therefore hopeless love for the actress Soledad Cordero, his death when he was as young as Byron or Chénier, make of Ignacio Rodríguez Galván the most moving figure of the lyric history of the country and the most interesting profile of its Romantic age. Reputed to be the initiator of Romanticism in Mexico, he envelops this new soul of expression in a national and rhythmical body, and offers the first example of sober and controlled assimilation of a foreign school in which so many, in so many countires, will commit excesses. He has only enough life for a few works. After *Muñoz, Inspector of Mexico,* he produces with mediocre results *The Viceroy's Favorite* in the old New Coliseum — now the Teatro Principal —, in 1842; he also writes *The Chapel* and *The Damned,* a drama which seems to have been known only to some of his friends; *The Guardian Angel,* which he is said not to have wanted published or performed. He figures in the Academy of San Juan de Letrán at the side of the most distinguished minds of his time, and he dies full of promise at the age of twenty-six.

His opposite in life and works is Fernando Calderón, a Romantic of the type who overdo themselves at the banquet table, adorned in French style with geographical exoticism, and the author of *The Tournament*; *Herman, or The Return From The Crusade*; and *Ann Boleyn,* whose titles are sufficiently illustrative. He also writes, besides many works performed in the provinces, *To None of The Three.*

Alonso de Avila, the only contribution of Guillermo Prieto to the theater, is produced at the Teatro Principal on the night of May 1, 1842, and — symbolically — misses the opportunity for success because of the appearance at the theater of Benito León Acosta, the first Mexican to successfully carry out, more or less, a daring balloon ascent. On the other hand, *Charles the Second The Bewitched,* by Gil y Zárate — performed on June 23 of the same year —, achieves the hard-won success of a hit in spite of its quality. On August 15, Ramón Navarrete y Landa produces his work *Emilia,* which was greeted with a "Wonderful, young man!" by the enigmatic literary pontiff Guillermo Prieto.

Authors arise gradually, frequently taking backward steps, stagnating, or more frequently taking no steps at all. In the year 1849 the five act drama *Valentina,* by Ignacio Anievas, who will later write *The Senator's Daughter or Political Hatred, Seduction* and other works whose theatrical worth is still unknown, is presented. The Cuban Juan Miguel Losada is the author of several works which can be included in Mexican dramatic production such as *The Shout of Dolores*; *Contrite, Unconfessed and a Martyr*; *A Star Behind a Cloud*; *The Return to the World*; *The Silken Cord.* About the same time (1850-1852) the fearless and fecund Pantaleón appears. His work· *Mexico City Cathedral* attains the glory of being, according to *El Siglo XIX,* "The best Mexican play produced during the season... That poor play holds the promise of better ones... The author should not write in verse... the poverty of his language can be heard in the extravagance and repetition of similar consonants... his lack of style is apparent in the many mistakes in each *redondilla.*" He writes several works : *The Children of Hernán Cortés or the Mexican Conspiracy* — naturally, always in verse —, *A Sublime Dishonor or Close to The Trojan Horse, The Glory of Grief* and *And For What Purpose?* So, why go on?

Works rain down such as *The Mysteries of Mexico,* by Niceto de Zamacois, such as "the Holy Biblical drama with grandiose trappings in the language of Cervantes," entitled *The Banquet of Baltasar or The Echo of The Devil*; such as *The Yankees in the Valley of Mexico.* Pablo Villaseñor, with his play *Clementina*; the fabricator of apotheosis Francisco Granados Maldonado, with *The Apotheosis of Iturbide*; Antonio M. Romero, with *The Corregidor of Guatemala,* all appear, and a healthy competition is established between a Pedro Díaz and Hilarión Frías, about whom it is said that the former wrote a play with the title *A Lightning Bolt and a Flower,* and the latter one entitled *A Flower and a Lightning Bolt.* In the year 1855, the same one in which the poet Zorrilla arrives in Mexico, José Tomás de Cuéllar associates himself with dramatic literature with his drama about social customs entitled *Obligations and Sacrifices,* to which he will add *The Disasters of An Attempt at Vengeance* and other plays. Under the pseudonym of Facundo, he is the first writer to concern himself profoundly with social matters ; he is a shrewd psychologist and, although limited by his times, he is quite transcendental, particularly in the novel, in which genre he has frequently been compared to Stendhal.

Following him come Francisco González Bocanegra, with *Vasco Núñez de Balboa*; the blind poet Juan Valle, with his only drama *Social Mysteries*; Juan A. Mateos and Vicente Riva Palacio, who initiate in 1861 their great theatrical offensive with *Hereditary Hate, Dangers of an Overcoat, Iturbide or The Embrace of Acatempan, Niagara Falls,* in addition to an interminable list of others. These two authors have an alarming fecundity, and both, but particularly Mateos, will utilize all the theatrical genres with the same intrepid abandon. Add to this such plays as *The Surrender of the Plaza of*

Puebla on March 22, 1856; *A Liberal Out of Necessity*; *An Episode on May Fifth*, an improvisation by a group of poets directed by Guillermo Prieto; the adaptation of *Women Be Damned!* by Luis G. Iza; *The Mill of Guadalajara*, a drama produced at the Teatro Principal "with cylinders and wheels moved by plain water," according to the programs; the works of Sebastián Movellán, Consul of Spain in Mexico (*The Anonymous One* and *A Drama at Home*); *The Empty House or Ghosts in Mexico*, by the obscure Carlota Contreras; the *zarzuela The Old Woman and The Grenadier*, with music by the Mexican Joaquín Luna... and shake well.

It would be possible to go on indefinitely. The truth is that little or nothing of all this is lasting or representative, that there is a constant sacrifice of the future for the present, and that generally the theater continues to be unappreciated, unknown and inaccessible.

Having mentioned those dramas and authors which constitute isolated and lofty entities in the cycle which stretches from Mexican Independence to 1867, carrying on their shoulders two empires and a shocking number of political struggles, there are the works that I mention and many more, which I refrain from citing because of discretion. Several translators and arrangers, among whom Alejandro Arango y Escandón deserves mention, work with greater or lesser activity. Authors are not lacking, but *homo passat ... et nec manet domus*. Criticism still has not appeared, and I find no work devoted to the study of the theater.

Later...

Fernando Orozco y Berra, author of the first romantic novel in Mexico (*The Thirty Years War*), also seems to have left several plays in the darkness and the disarray of theatrical production in the past century, a disarray and darkness which only between 1870 and 1880 renounce their long inherited labors. The theater finally reaches legal age and produces, however briefly, the impression of becoming crystallized in a more uniform and symmetrical existence and of having an awareness of itself.

From that time forward a long parade of authors files across the numerous Mexican stages; Jesús Echaiz, Enrique de Olavarría y Ferrari, a Spaniard and naturalized Mexican, Manuel Peredo, Justo Sierra (*Pity*), Manuel Acuña (*The Past*); Antonio Guillén y Sánchez, Isabel Prieto de Landázuri, José Rosas Moreno, Manuel María Romero, Joaquín Villalobos, Hipólito Serán, Francisco Ortiz, Rafael de Zayas Enríquez, Francisco A. Lerdo, José Monroy, Ramón Manterola, Roberto Esteva, José Peón y Contreras, Alberto Bianchi, Antonio Zavala, Ildefonso Estrada y Zenea, Juan de Dios Peza, José María Vigil, Carlos Escudero, Alfredo Chavero, Agapito Silva, Mariana Peñaflores de Silva, Luis Muñoz Ledo, Adolfo M. Obregón, whose drama *The Hand of God* in three acts and prose is referred to, for some unknown reason, as the finest work of its kind; Vicente Morales, Ignacio Herrera de León, Miguel Portillo, José de Jesús Cuevas, Manuel José Othón, Julio Espinosa, Eduardo Noriega, Manuel Pérez Bibbins, Leopoldo Cano, Francisco Gutiérrez Solórzano, Gonzalo Larrañaga, Vicente Morales, Manuel Puga y Acal, Apolinar Castillo, Ricardo Domínguez, in an error, Manuel Gutiérrez Nájera; José R. del Castillo, Felipe Haro, Victoria González, Portilla y Monteleone, Javier Sánchez, Tomás Villanueva y Serrano, Antonio de P. Moreno, Manuel Calderón, Ramón Arriola, Alfonso Rodríguez and Federico Gamboa, whose work *The Last Campaign* signals the beginning of Naturalism.

It might seem that the list is interminable. It is an enormous group arranged as chronologically as possible, which covers thirty years of theatrical activity without any direction or any school, with the exception of the Romantics, in which some writers produce innumerable works which are not published and which are lost in the wanderings of the theatrical archives; others produce only one play or a patriotic, detective, or social sketch; many produce poor plays whose production is inexplicable; others produce adaptations and deformations of foreign works, and only some few have a definitive and extended career.

The praiseworthy ones are:

Isabel Prieto de Landázuri, because she is, after Juana de Asbaje, the first Mexican woman who writes for the theater (*A Lily Among Thorns*);

José Rosas Moreno, whose works (*The Relatives, A Plan for Divorce, Daily Bread*) contain, with the possible exception of *Sor Juana Inés de la Cruz,* all his personality which shows such fondness for simple things and the home and childhood and, further, the clear imprint of his careful hand and his well controlled artistic drive. With his plays *The New Year, A Geography Lesson* and *Filial Love,* he marks the beginning of the written children's theater in Mexico. Perhaps his best work is *The Bard of Acolhuacán,* a lyrical

dramatization of the life of Netzahualcóyotl, which was never published, as Luis González Obregón kindly informs me;

José Peón y Contreras. His fecundity damages him and he is
forced at times to produce his works anonymously, as is the case
with *Struggles of Honor and Love* (staged on July 6, 1876). He is
recognized, however, for "Peón will always emerge because of his
beautiful verses, because of his extremely short acts, and because
of his plot..." Luis G. Urbina calls him "The favorite son of the
sixteenth century," and for him he "is above all a playwright of
the old school, a dreamer, a sentimentalist and a rhetorician." He
makes a reality, specifically, of the theatrical specialist, who is so
rare in Mexico. Struggling with his era, he has the merit of searching,
like Rodríguez Galván, for a national outlet for his production, and
for living within the theatrical sphere while following the classical
traditions. His play *The Daughter of the King* is, doubtlessly together with *Antón de Alaminos,* more than just the best of his
personal works, the best of the Romantic harvest in the nation.
Núñez de Arce is said to have found encouragement in his works,
"inventiveness, facility with dialogue, and passion when it is necessary." It is true, however, that apart from these qualities Peón y
Contreras lacks what distinguishes the dramatist from the poet and
the novelist. That is to say, the ability to inject personality into
a character and not character into a personality. That is theater.
His works might be called a musical composition with only the
melody, they are incomplete and are, therefore, "a group of archaic
well-rhymed fables." If he had been able to unite his constancy with
a more sceptical spirit, a less immediate psychology and a cosmic
philosophy, he would have been a lesser poet but a greater dramatist,
perhaps the greatest dramatist since Alarcón;

Alberto Bianchi, because he perceives the theater in its primordial aspect as a great tribunal which, ancient and modern genius
aside, does not seem to have been understood in Spain by the
theatrical public. His work *Martyrs of the People,* which the critic
of *El Monitor* calls the "candid picture of the gimmick, the most
odious crime of our rulers," because of its success at the box-office,
won for him a sentence of one year in prison during the twisted
finale of the government of Sebastián Lerdo de Tejada (1876);

Manuel José Othón, because he is in the provinces where he is
insensitive to the influences which occur, and with roots of an admi-

rable poetic clarity, also lives within the theater, busies himself with it and observes it while placing under the control of his attention that artistic patience which makes him stand out in lyric poetry as well, and which he does not confuse with the theater. Although lifted by contemporary criticism to the level of Juan Ruiz de Alarcón, he is indubitably close to Manuel Eduardo de Gorostiza in the scope of his vision, even if in a different genre.

I have intentionally left this anachronistic and isolated space for José Martí, a journalist and member of the Alarcón Society in which José Peón y Contreras and Roberto Esteva figured, and whose play *Love is Repaid with Love* was produced by the Spanish actor Enrique Guasp de Peris in 1876.

In all the rest the factor prevails, which is common in Mexico because of what may be called a lack of professionalism, that permits the creation of one play or a hundred without this being equivalent to one's being a playwright, since such a motive does not evolve under a harmonious and profound discipline and consequently does not reach a balance of experience. When it is not this, it is an incomprehensible mixture of genres: Sunday promenades through the *zarzuela,* the operetta, the *pastorela,* a magic show with paraphernalia, the revue, the comedy or the tragedy, however the sun dawns. Self-restraint is the second element in art after the creative faculty.

We have suffered since then from cases such as the adaptations of *The Hunchback* of Paul Féval, done in verse by Olavarría y Ferrari in one week; such as *The Missionaries of Love,* by the same author, "done on the basis of the French work which has served in our times as a libretto for the widely acclaimed and repeatedly performed zarzuela *The Musketeers in the Convent* — it is certain that the former created a scandal even if it was not a success —; such as *Don Fernando The Condemned,* a "rough dramatic sketch" by Justo Sierra and Enrique Olavarría, which the authors never permitted to be published — which must have been due to Justo Sierra —; such as the adaptations of *Les Misérables* and *The Laughing Man* done by Juan A. Mateos. In this same show-case should be mentioned *The Black Venus* by the same Olavarría who "was not familiar when I wrote it with... *La Vénus Noire* of M. A. Belcot and I created it whimsically in four days"; *The Blackbird,* by Juan A. Mateos, "who took from Leon Gazlan the idea for his play," and *The Father of the Six Monkeys or The Prophet of the Rock,* a burlesque organized for the theater by Juan de Dios Peza, Baz and "other wits" concerning the prophecy of Nicolás de Zúñiba y Miranda which did not occur on August 11, 1887.

At any rate, this uniform and continuous movement causes, particularly between the years 1870 and 1880 — finally — the appearance of critics of literary quality whose lead will be followed later, among whom Manuel Gutiérrez Nájera and Luis G. Urbina are the best and most original, even if some are more conversationalists than critics.

Later, we find Alberto Michel — author, translator and adapter —, Rafael Medina, Aurelio González Carrasco and José F. Elizondo in minor genres like the *zarzuela*; the latter also in the revue, although much later.

Still in the nineteenth century, but belonging to our era and to our concerns, Marcelino Dávalos and José Joaquín Gamboa appear. The latter is a nationalist and revolutionary who is the archtype of the Mexican author, although lacking in foresight, and he is the first to bring to the stage the pressing social problems of the nation; later he will lose his direction and will not, in my view, completely develop himself. The former, with plays and theatrical criticism, will dedicate himself to this art until his death (January 29, 1931), maintaining himself always at a certain literary level and leaving behind a work which, of all those he wrote, was certainly the one which he did best: *The Knight, Death, and The Devil,* inspired by the engraving of Albrecht Dürer. It is necessary to point out, however, that this work, staged on January 9, 1931 by the Rambal troupe, is similar in title to that of the dramatic poem "The Knight, Death, and The Devil" by the South American writer César E. Arroya which was performed at the Sucre Theater, in Quito prior to 1930, and "with great success."

After the previously mentioned operas and *The Empty House,* composed in Mexico City by Maestro Lauro Rossi and produced between 1831 and 1835, the opera appears in the spotlight again in the second half of the nineteenth century; Luis Baca composes *Leonor,* during his stay in France, based on a libretto by Carlo Bozzeti and — later — *Juana of Castile,* based on a libretto by the

Florentine Temístocles Solera; on September 29, 1859 — birthday
of President Miramón — Cenobio Paniagua stages his *Catalina de
Guisa,* with libretto by Félix Romani, and in 1863 (May 5), *Pietro
D'Avano.* The success of *Catalina de Guisa* inspires "a blood uncle
of Adelina Patti," who is apparently named Antonio Barilli, to
compose *A Walk in Santa Anita,* based on a libretto of José Casa-
nova and Víctor Landaluce (1859). Octaviano Valle presents *Clotilde
de Coscensa* (July 19, 1863); Mateo Torres Serrato performs *The
Two Fóscari,* with the same libretto used by G. Verdi (November
11, 1863), and later *Fidelio,* which is supposedly inspired by Beethoven; *Pirro of Aragon,* composed by Leonardo Canales, is presented on July 12, 1864; there is also the work known as *Adelaida
and Comingio,* a composition by Ramón Vega, whose opera *The
Queen of León* seems to have been produced in January, 1871 by
the Catholic Society of Mexico, and a *Don Quixote of La Mancha,*
by Miguel Planas, with lyrics by A. García, performed with the
title *Don Quixote at The Enchanted Inn* on May 5, 1871, at
the Teatro Nacional; Melesio Morales is the author of *Romeo and
Juliet,* with libretto by Félix Romani adapted by Bellini, Vacai
and Berliva, performed on January 27, 1863 at the Teatro Nacional;
of *Ildegonda,* produced in 1865 in the then Teatro Imperial by the
opera company of Biacchi, concerning which I will say more later;
of *Charlemagne, Gino Corssini* — written in Europe and of which
the former remains unpublished —; of *The Tempest* and *The
Wandering Jew* — unpublished —; of *Cleopatra* (1891) and *Anita,*
libretto by Enrique Golisciani which is only announced in 1903.
Miguel Meneses composes *Agorante, King of Nubia,* which is performed at the Teatro Imperial on July 6, 1864, the birthday of
Maximilian of Hapsburg, who attends in company of the Empress;
The Fairy of the Lake; Judith; Louise de Lavalliere, and the lyric
drama *Atala. The Last Thought of Weber,* a lyrical-dramatic composition by Julio Ituarte, with lyrics by Luis Muñoz Ledo, is
performed in 1869. On September 13, 1871, Aniceto Ortega stages
his opera *Guatimozín.* After a respite, in 1892, *Columbus in Santo
Domingo,* by Julio M. Morales, the son of Melesio, fails, and in
1893 (July 31), *Keofar* by Felipe Villanueva, who had recently died,
is presented at the Teatro Principal coinciding with the installation
of a "splendid set of electric lights." In the same year Ricardo
Castro composes his *Don Juan of Austria,* which is never performed.

The majority of these composers are distinguished, have a fine musical background, and were respected in Europe as brilliant artists.

The *zarzuela* and the operetta are equally cultivated genres, even if only with little intensity in the early periods because of the torrent of Spanish plays. The pastoral *zarzuela* in three acts entitled *The Sons of Bato and Bras or The Devil's Mischief,* by Mariano Osorno (1856), can be mentioned with the pastoral operetta *The Happiest Night or The Rewards of Innocence* (1863) and *A Troubled Soul,* with libretto by Olona with music by the Mexican actor Felipe Suárez (1867). In 1870 the imitations of the European variety shows introduced by Eduardo González appear for the first time. The first is *The Revue of 1869,* performed on January 30, 1870, with lyrics by Olavarría y Ferrari and music by Melesio Morales, who did not dare to sign it. *The Page of the Vicereine,* a libretto by Alfredo Chavero with music by José Austri (1879), *A Fiesta in Santa Anita,* with lyrics by Juan de Dios Peza and music by Luis Arcaraz (1886); *Fears and Pleasures,* with libretto by Ernesto González and music by Julio Ituarte (1887), are all worthy of mention. On the other hand, it appears that between 1890 and 1892 several Mexican *zarzuelas* are performed. As composers in this genre the Mexican José Austri and the Spaniard Luis Arcaraz, who really comes to belong to Mexico, stand out particularly, both of whom, either in collaboration or separately, write music for several librettos of Spanish and Mexican authors such as Aguirre del Pino, Juan A. Mateos, Liern, Pina y Domínguez, Miguel Echegaray, Alfredo Chavero, Ramos Carrión and Vital Aza, Olavarría, Peza y Perrín and Palacios.

Reverse

Having described the obverse side of the theatrical coin in the nineteenth century, the abundance of actors now requires me to describe the reverse side. The actors are beginning to become dignified and to figure among the reasons for public attention. It is true that they are not specialists and that actors and actresses, in order to live, must be at the same time dancers and — repulsive term — professional singers.

Their names and their salaries — which do not yet approach the quantities in Hollywood — are already widely publicized, and Vic-

torio Rocamora, "musical leading man," the leading ladies Luz
Vallecillo and Agustina Montenegro, stand out; the "leading *gracioso*" Luciano Cortés; the "exceptional" Fernando Gavila, who
is the author of works such as *American Loyalty,* a heroic drama
in one act, and *The Pretty Country Girl,* a *zarzuela* in two acts;
Dolores Munguía, Josefa García, Andrés Castillo (singers), and Guadalupe Gallardo, Magdalena Lupert, Isabel Rendón and Juan Ma-
rini, "dancers," besides others who were members of the company,
were noteworthy. Moreover, from the end of the eighteenth century
onward the feudal custom of theatrical family dynasties begins and
is the reason for the failure of the conservatories, whose products
are always considered to be intruders. To cite only one case, Juan
Marami, a descendent of the Jerónimo of the same last name who
figures in the annals of the previous century, may be mentioned.
And so it will go, as in the Biblical curses, into the fourth and
fifth generations.

The lyric custom of the time — is there a better adjective? —
leads to the eulogizing of artists in verse, as in the case of Luz de
Vallecillo and Luciano Cortés, who are praised in a sonnet "A
Certain Finger" (*El Diario,* October 19, 1807).

The theater, of course, exploits the social and political events
of the times, a custom which will retard theatrical autonomy sever-
ely. The reporter who recounts the series of celebrations held in
Mexico to solemnize the proclamation of King Ferdinand VII does
not mention the name of the play performed on that occasion in the
Coliseum — is it of any consequence? —; but he indicates that in
the presentation the "famous actor" Luciano Cortés and the "best
dancemaster we have had at this Court," Juan Medina, even though
they were not active in the theater, played parts. "It is useless to
expand upon the lighting of the patio and theater efforts of the
actors, and other similar things, which are to be expected, but their
emotion and the enthusiasm with which the *zorzicos* were heard,
which befitted the surroundings and had been composed that very
day and which Dolores Munguía, Andrés Castillo and Victoria
Rocamora sang, "the second having given his word to his wife that
he would never return to the stage," all should not be omitted. The
birthday of the King, in October, 1808, is also celebrated at the Coliseum, "and Luciano Cortés and Luz Vallecillo, who returned to
the theater on such a memorable day to continue to flatter us

with the profferings of such a useful trade for society, took part in the performance."

The public which gathers at the theater naturally undergoes those emotional crises which are common to the multitudes of any genre; in it political news and enthusiasm reach a sublime diapason of sonority, and things are accomplished through the nervous system which could not be done by means of persuasion in the same way that something can be achieved through tears which cannot be accomplished by sentiment.

On the other hand, the diversity of spectacles begins to become necessary, and among those imported at first is The Royal Equestrian Circus of Phillipe Lailson, which appears in 1808. In 1810 (June 25) Dr. José Beye de Cisneros is honored by the theatrical company on the occasion of his election as a deputy to the Cortes representing the capital city of the colony.

During the struggle for social change the monarchical government, administrator of the theater, must have had realistic sketches performed which were dually intended to introduce into a false spring the already invernal submission of the people and to caricature the national political bosses. Doubtlessly also the victories won over the insurgents were announced there in order to impress the public to the highest degree.

In April, 1817 the management of the Coliseum is in the hands of the artists Luciano Cortés, José María Amador, José Antonio Herrera, José Agustín Spetali, Andrés del Castillo and Agustina Montenegro, "who had been living in the country for more than ten years." The period of the lease was for three years, and at the first performance (April 6) *The Boyhood of the Cid,* by Guillén de Castro, is presented.

The year 1819 is outstanding because of the event which consists of the arrival of the Spanish actor Juan López Extremera, also a dramatist and author of the five act tragedy *Inés de Castro* and of the play *The Pirates in the Forest of the Sepulchers.* Apart from minor details — such as these plays having been criticized by a member of "The Friends of Good Taste," an association of the most cultured patrons of the Coliseum, who speaks of the "accursed Romantic taste" and "Corruptor Kotzebue," and the author's having followed his suggestions by modifying the aforementioned tragedy — there is nothing else until Independence.

Things change by then, becoming the omnipresent opposite extreme. Nationalism is becoming generalized in the country and, after the erection of the first open air pavillion in Latin America, anti-Spanish and patriotic plays of circumstance take over the theater. Actors and actresses, in the casts of the programs, become members of the citizenry, incorporating themselves into the new reality which will permit them to earn a living. They continue to be foreigners for the most part; but they have already provided themselves with a letter of residence on the national stages. They continue, furthermore, to be backward and far from specialization. It is true that the peculiar melomania of the diverse Mexican publics is satiated by the relative nourishment of the opera and the *zarzuela,* and that these genres are the best guarantee of subsistence for the actors. The custom of inserting dramatic *entremeses,* dances, and popular songs into the dramatic performances will be prolonged until the early part of the twentieth century in which, with unimportant differences, those variations will persist. Apparently there is no renovation or initiative on the part of managements. The theater under those conditions is beginning to become a habit, if not for the public at least for the actors. It is said that at the time Independence was won there was a crisis in Mexico, a crisis in the matter of sets and "very capable actors who can perform our best plays with accuracy" (*Semanario Político y Literario).* Nevertheless, the same weekly, with a journalistically academic criterion, later requested that works of Moratín, Lope de Vega, Quintana, Calderón de la Barca, Moreto, etc., be performed. In fact these works were not necessary, even though the scant education of the actors, which is reflected in the audience — which is nothing more than a mirror — meant that the sensitive and truculent works which have come down to the present period, as a refuge for that particular class which represents the immobile part of humanity, might have been more enjoyable. The poems in praise of the actors — actors who I hope were better than the poems — are not lacking, and one of them is directed in tribute to an actor named Aragón, an interpreter of William Hamlet Shakespeare.

In the year 1822 (October), the actor Luciano Cortés establishes himself in a theater situated in the "pit which was for cocks," in competition with the Coliseum. Cecilia Ortiz, reputed to be very attractive and gracious, and the actors Torremocha and Amador, all of whom receive applause in *The Delinquent Honored,* follow him. In the same year the Coliseum ceases its dependence on the Royal Hospital for Illegitimates and passes into the hands of the city government, which from that time on takes charge of its management and leasing.

Rare things happen such as the act of treason, at least in the title, committed against Voltaire in his *Alzire* — which, if I am not mistaken, made of him the first author called to the stage to receive public acclaim — and which is known in Mexico by the title *Elmira.*

The actor Diego María Garay — a Spaniard, so as not to have to mention it further — is introduced in July, 1824 in the tragedy *The Knights Templar.* A little later he undertakes a campaign of "defanaticization," and performs works such as *Virtue Pursued by Superstition and Fanaticism; Inside the Inquisition,* whose suspension was ordered, and *Charles IX, or The School for Kings.* In his troupe María Pautret is outstanding. In the same year a prestidigitator named Castelli appears on the scene.

Several events particularly stand out in 1825. Mariano Elízaga found the Philharmonic Conservatory, or Society, the first of its kind in the country, on April 18 on Escalerillas Street. The Gallos Theater, also referred to as the Provisional or Las Moras, is rebuilt and reopened on August 21 by a troupe in which Andrés Castillo or del Castillo, Andrés García and Manuela García Gamborino figure; finally, Ministers Poinsett and Ward arrive in Mexico. A new passion takes control of public opinion which is attributable to the installation, as a result of the diplomatic gestures of the aforementioned ministers, of the Scottish Rite and York Rite Masonic Lodges, the latter having been founded by José María Alpuche e Infante. The proportional machiavellianism of Minister Poinsett concludes happily with the splitting of the factions, which is duplicated in salons and families and even among theatrical people themselves. Their private lives have their classical hour of intrigue and envy. Let us be gentle and discreet and leave aside the superficial and biting collection of anecdotes in this regard.

The Barber of Seville by Rossini is performed at the Provisional Theater on February 23, 1826 by Castillo and Andrés Pautret. In the same year, provided with a recommendation by Manuel Eduardo de Gorostiza, who was at that time Consul of

Mexico in the Low Countries, the Spanish actor Andrés Prieto arrives in the capital, and it is said that he was superb. Against him Diego María Garay conspires; he is attacked, furthermore, because he is a Spaniard, and he receives the bitter criticism of the Cuban poet José María de Heredia. Prieto defends himself through his work. In his repertory are *Tartuffe, or The Hypocrite; The Café; Pardon for All; The Mayor of Zalamea; Othello or The Moore of Venice*; he performs Mexican works such as the tragedy *Selim,* by Luis Antepara, on August 1, which seems to have been terrible; on October 14 he arranges the debut of Guadalupe Munguía, a Mexican actress, who does very well as Paquita in *The Maidens' Consent,* and, reconciled with Heredia, he performs his tragedy *The Turmoil* on January 8, 1827. This same year contains the performance of Rossini's *Othello* at the Provisional Theater of Andrés del Castillo; and — a notable event — the presentation on June 29, in *The Barber of Seville,* of the famous Manuel García. The singing of the Indian sirens now reaches such artistic celebrities. With it, as well as with all its family, come its offspring: Viardot and Malibran, who later moves Alfred de Musset to tears. In their company Rita de Santa Marta, Waldeck and La Pelligrini are outstanding; but it is the wrong moment; in short, they are a failure.

The atmosphere of revulsion for Spaniards, which has been growing since 1821, culminates with their expulsion from the country and, naturally, empties the theaters. Among those expelled is the actor Miguel Valleto, who nevertheless will return to Mexico to remain until his death. Andrés Prieto, excluded from expulsion, continues working; in his troupe is the now legendary Agustina Montenegro, and in 1829 he arranges for the Mexican actress Soledad Cordero, who is loved so deeply by Ignacio Rodríguez Galván, to have her debut at her side.

Foreign artistic intervention takes on, little by little, a definitely formal character. It is the Spanish actors particularly who will give life to the traditional concept of Mexico as a second homeland, and they will remain here through their children in some cases down to the present time, a theatrical *criollismo* thus being formed which has not generally been beneficial for the country.

Would it be appropriate, without delaying too much, to glance at the theatrical map which entertains Mexico during the nineteenth century?

There are Spanish dramatic troupes like the one of Bernardo de Avecilla, which is not well received (1831); Italian opera companies, like the one headed by Filippo Galli and Carolina Pellegrini; magicians and hypnotists; physicians like Mr. Perinor, who is featured at the new theater on Zuleta Street (1931); operas like *Agnese*, by Paer, which is a failure; *The Secret Marriage*, by Cimarrosa, which so pleased Stendhal and which was also a success here (1832); and *The Empty House*, composed in Mexico by Maestro Lauro Rossi and performed between 1831 and 1835. There are plays by Gorostiza such as *Bread and Onions with You*, performed in 1833; works such as the "famous tragedy" *The Compensation of Greed by The Indian Woman Tepoczina or Two Victims Immolated by the Oppressive Tyrant*, and the play *The Eclipsed Sun of Italy and The Dawning Sun over Our Land or The Miraculous Appearance of Our Lady of The Remedies*, which I believe to be of nationalistic affiliation; there is the "Great Cosmorama," built on Plateros Street — this recalls the Vautrinorama of Balzac in 1833-1834; the translation by Gorostiza of *The Step-Mother*, in which the Mexican actor Antonio Caso has his debut (1834); there is the first attempt at a balloon ascent and — of course — the first notable failure, by Adolphe Théodore (1834), and another by Robertson, who is said to be the man who introduced electroplating into France (1835); Albini de Vellani has her debut in the opera (1836), and — novelty of novelties — there is the debut of the industrious and wise fleas (1837). Jean Baptiste Montrésor strengthens the opera in 1838, the same year in which Antonio Castro and Soledad Cordero, together with Fuentes, Salgado, Palomera, La Dubreville, and La Platero, all organized into a troupe, devote themselves to producing foreign works such as *The Fat Man*, by Bretón, and *Angelo, Tyrant of Padua*, by the great and encyclopedic Victor Hugo. There are Mexican works among all of these: *Muñoz, Inspector of Mexico; A Tyrant Like Any Other*, a parody of the work by Hugo which provokes uprisings among the people, who are less accustomed to this type of play than present-day audiences.

Further: there are aerostatic ascents by Louis A. Lauriat; phrenological experiments by Professor Albert Baily (sic); the inauguration of new theaters: the Nuevo México is opened on May 30, 1841 with a company headed by Francisco Pineda, who is said to be a great actor, and Fernando Martínez, both Spaniards, and among the actresses Concepción Molino and Eduwiges Ramos. At the performance *The Tournament,* by Calderón, and *Edward's Sons,* by Casimir Delavigne in the translation by Bretón de los Herreros, are done together.

In the Coliseum — later the Teatro Principal — Miguel Valleto, Soledad Cordero and La Dubreville perform in works such as *Marino Faliero;* the Italian opera, for the usual reasons, takes refuge in the Teatro de los Gallos with *Lucía de Lammermoor* starring Anaida Castellan de Giampetro (1841).

Among the publications of the period, *El Apuntador* seems to have been superior, within its field, to *Mosaic* and to the *Semanario de Las Señoritas.* Casimiro del Collado, Andrés Quintana Roo, J. M. Lafragua, José Joaquín Pesado, Alejandro Arango y Escandón, José Gómez de la Cortina and others contribute to it. In the face of the theatrical situation in Mexico *El Apuntador* is coldly suppressed, publishing in its last issue (on November 30, 1841) a — shall I say a somewhat droll? — last will and testament through which it bequeathed the bitterest and most ironic advice to actors, actresses and empresarios. About the same time *El Siglo XIX* appears.

If the placing of the cornerstone of the Gran Teatro Nacional on February 18, 1842, by the protective hand of President Santa-Anna, raises hope for a change in the comic life of the country, the same absurd things nevertheless continue to happen. In spite of the works of Gorostiza, a sign of modernity (*Paulina*), of those of Calderón (*To None of the Three, Herman or the Return from the Crusade*) and of the works of Ignacio Rodríguez Galván (*The Viceroy's Favorite*), which are produced at the Principal, the Nuevo México attracts the public with the magic of *The Goat's Foot.* The literary theater is of almost no consequence, and the great national actors are still far distant.

There is La Ricci in the opera; María Cañete, the so-called "Thalia of Havana," and Guillermo Prieto, a singer in that epicene genre which consisted of the *tonadilla* and a play; Josefa Galindo de Martínez and Rosa Peluffo, all foreigners, are on the stage. Antonio Castro begins to restrict himself in *The Belly Laugh,* and will distinguish himself with his characterization of the popular Don Simplicio Bobadilla Majaderano y Cabeza de Buey. In the Nuevo México the Spanish dance company of the Pavías is featured, and another small location for spectacles is inaugurated in 1843 with the name Teatro de la Unión or Puente Quebrado.

The concert artist, uncommon until then, begins to arrive with greater abundance in the nation. A concert by the cellist Maximilian Bohrer, from Munich, is the first performance offered by the Teatro de Santa-Anna on the occasion of its opening on February 10, 1844; in the Teatro Nuevo México on February 22 the Belgian violinist Henri Vieuxtemps has his debut.

Another theater, the Puerto Nuevo, specializes in the *pastorela*: *The Happiest Night or The Reward of Innocence; Michael and Lucifer, Shepherds with Opposing Opinions; Noah's Ark in The Mountains of Armenia; The Arcadia in Bethlehem or The Loves of Felizardo*; the Principal, insecure in spite of having Castro, Salgado — a Mexican disciple of Andrés Prieto —, Soledad Cordero, La Dubreville and La Francesconi, presents allegorical plays (*There are Dreams which are Lessons of The Effects of Deception*) and plays with magic like the fine *The Goat's Foot; Martha The Wanderer* and *Jane The Shorttailed or The Wonder of Jerez,* which were sometimes national and sometimes foreign.

The theatrical season of the Teatro de Santa-Anna begins on April 7, 1844. A discreet program announces that the paraphernalia play *A Glass of Water* will be performed "together with, for the first time, the three act play *The Walls Have Ears,* the composition of a Mexican." Poor Alarcón! According to Guillermo Prieto the work of that Mexican did not please the public. The competition between the theater embraces nicknames and other things; the Principal calls the Nuevo México "an old enclosure belonging to Belchite," and the Nuevo México calls the Principal "the cemetery of Santa Paula," allusions to the sites on which both theaters are located.

In the same year, 1844, as a result of political agitation, the flattering statue of Antonio López de Santa-Anna which stood in the portico of the theater was pulled down with the name removed from it and placed temporarily in the portico on the street on which it was found (Vergara), and later (on December 15) in the doorway at the Gran Teatro Nacional. In it busts of authors and Mexican actors are placed, and in it is performed for our stage, on December 7 of that same year, *Don Juan Tenorio,* which belongs irretrievably to Mexico. The bust of Fernando Calderón is placed there on July 11, 1845.

Let us point out the presence of Eufrasia Borghese (1845) in the opera and that of Carmen Corcuera in the drama (1846). The regulations which control the theater are imperfect; but the reforms which are proposed are worse. The proposal presented by Lafragua, Espinosa de los Monteros and Larralde to the city council which contained, among other statements, one to the effect that "the Council itself would approve plays and would be empowered to correct them," and so on (1846), may be cited.

Dramatic societies are established such as the one presided over by Josefa and Remedios Amador, in whose undertakings the author Francisco Granados Maldonado figures, among others, and it occupies the building of the Lancaster Society on Betlemitas Street. Preceded by the *quintillas* of Bretón de los Herreros, which are about to be interpreted as offensive to Mexico, the "very distinguished and beautiful young lady" Isabel Luna has her debut in *The Lovers of Teruel* at the Nacional in 1846. Some companies leave the theaters, and others come to them. There is no specialization implicit in that, and we still have no dramatic theater or operatic theater. There are mountebanks who appear at the Teatro Nacional, which had recently been abandoned by the opera or the drama, such as the Turon, Armant and Duverloy Company.

The political events of the times, on the other hand, which are no longer of a familiar and internal character, close the theaters and impose silence on the city. A little after the entrance of General Quitmann into Mexico City (September 14, 1847), a group of American actors takes possession of the Teatro Nacional and, on the twenty-ninth of the same month, *The Lady of the Lyons or Love and Pride* is performed. However, on October 3 the Great Spanish Dramatic Company begins again its work in that theater, and that night's performance includes, among several numbers, a song by María Cañete. Be it history or an anecdote, it happened that two assistants of General Scott go, on instructions from him, to María Cañete and Rosa Peluffo to request the reopening of the theater by the troupe to which both belong. Rosa Peluffo refuses; but María Cañete accepts, with the object of helping the Mexicans by offering to point out to the leader of the invaders which persons among the numerous prisoners are patriots and which are simple evildoers. She is named adviser for this reason and it is said that she left a profound impression upon General Scott. Later attacked for her conduct, she is defended by *El Monitor Republicano*: "She kept many from being flogged because of her influence and efforts; she kept others from being punished and being fined as well; and the second time when she was able to have the execution of Luz Vega postponed ("who was a true patriot and noted Republican"), Miss Cañete's efforts were such that we find difficulty describing them. Let it only be said that we admire what she did and that no Mexican woman could have done more."

On December 16, 1847, at thirty years of age, Soledad Cordero, who was apparently at least the most brilliant theatrical promise in this first half of the century, died in Zacatecas. Her funeral, according to the record, was held with great pomp and solemnity.

Magicians and ventriloquists reach down to our times: Alexander Herr brings "a new machine for producing children" and makes a litle girl come forth from an egg; Giovanni Rossi, of the same profession, holds forth in company with a dancer named Fanny Martin (1848). The exchange of ratifications between the United States and Mexico having been effected on May 30, 1848, the theaters which had remained closed — the Principal and the Nuevo México — are opened again on June 1, and with the departure of the North Americans on June 12, the entire city plunges itself into celebrations. *Marguerite of Burgundy* or *The Tower of Nesle,* which even in 1932 will exercise its fatal influence at the Teatro Hidalgo, is performed with great success.

A new hope for the dramatic art arises in 1849. Its name is Dorotea López; a certain J. M. L. dedicates an ode to her and she is, in the opinion of *El Siglo XIX,* "the only Mexican actress of some present merit and with not a little hope for the future." She disappears later, however.

The celebrities continue coming; Mexico is a suitable country for it. The English soprano Ana Bishop and the pianist Henry Herz figure among the performers of the year 1849. With the first came Alfred Bablot, whose destiny was in Mexico, and the second composed a Mexican national anthem for the contest organized by the Academy in August of that year. Theaters of no consequence arise, such as the Pabellón Mexicano on Arsinas Street, and, also in 1849, the Monplaisir dance company appears, which includes among its great number *The Caliph of Baghdad, Esmeralda or Our Lady of Paris* — with music by Pugni — and *The Triumph of the Cross,* which left a delightful memory. There is an incessant flow of material, then, which keeps alive the body of the theater in Mexico; but it has no influence whatsoever on its mind for, to the contrary, it impedes its elevation.

On January 31, 1849, for the benefit of Manuela Francesconi, an arrangement made by a Mexican of the first part of the *Montecristo* is performed at the Teatro Nacional, with the honored guest playing the role of Edmund Dantès. Besides being bad the adaptation is too long, it goes past midnight, and the terrible rumor circulates to the effect that the audience entered the theater in January and came out in February.

Verdi comes to Mexico with *Hernani* (1850); but the sensation of the year is *The Three Musketeers,* performed in four nights. The cornerstone of the Teatro Iturbide is laid; at the Nacional the bust of Manuel Eduardo de Gorostiza is placed... And in the theater?

Eufrasia Amat, later known as "the Mexican linnet," appears in 1852 (July 26), presented by the operatic company to which Balbina Steffenone belongs. In the first half of that year the first attempt at the founding of a dramatic conservatory is made, whose direction is entrusted to the Spanish actor José Cejudo. His death, in 1853, carries both to the grave. Also in 1853, Antonio López de Santa-Anna returns, now as His Serene Highness, in both the theater and in government. The Teatro de Oriente still... had Spanish actors: Juan de Mata Ibarzábal... There is the life and death of Henrietta Sontag, Countess Rossi, who is attacked by *cholera morbus* (1854)... There are plays by Gertrudis Gómez de Avellaneda (*The Adventurers*)... There is Matilde Díez, who performs some Mexican works: *The Seduction,* by Anievas; *To None of the Three,* by Calderón; *Obligations and Sacrifices,* by José Tomás de Cuéllar (1855)... There are pastoral *zarzuelas*... And, of course, there are plays by Pantaleón Tovar.

This museum now shows us a "Great Aerial Theater in the Temple of Thundering Jupiter"; the debut of the Spanish actress Josefa García; national operas; the Teatro de la Esmeralda; the conversion of the Teatro Fama into the Teatro Hidalgo, with gas lighting for the first time.

Finally one figure arises. It is true that she belongs to music because music has been cultivated with greater intensity than the drama. But she is the first interpretive star. Nothing has been so universal in Mexico before, nor as unique, as are the two extremes of the art. Angela Peralta appears as Leonora in *Il Trovatore* in the year 1860 (July 18), in a performance organized by the Association of Saint Vincent de Paul; a performance whose lyric half is directed by the sonorous José Zorrilla. What a day of rest in this monotonous week of labor. The voice of Angela Peralta, according to those who heard her, embellished it prodigiously.

Afterwards will come the French, who will make of the Iturbide a "Théatre de l'Armée" or "L'Eldorado," and they will present vaudevilles like *The Loves of Cleopatra* and *The Sleepwalker*; there are the balloon ascents, which are destined to become legendary, of Joaquín de la Cantolla y Rico; the opera of Biacchi; the Teatro Nacional, whose collection of busts has increased with that of the actor Antonio Castro, will be renamed the Imperial; the equestrian circus of Chiarini will enter into competition with the opera of Adelina Murio-Celli; in the Duclos-Ortiz dramatic company the Mexican María de Jesús Servín will have her debut, and the incident at the Hill of Bells and the madness of Carlota Amalia of Belgium will take place; Concha Méndez will refuse to sing the song "Mamá Carlota" merely to satisfy the amused ferocity of the public, and it will be worth a pension from the royal house of Austria to her; José Valero and Salvadora Cairón, who several times will exalt the states of Mexico (1868), will arrive, and *The Truth Suspected*, performed at the Teatro Principal in a tribute to Juan Ruiz de Alarcón, will not please the public either. For some time a young actor has been emerging, Gerardo López del Castillo, who in 1867 takes over the direction of the dramatic company of the recently founded Mexican Liceo, of which he is also the leading actor.

The can-can, introduced in 1869 by the Gaztambide Troupe, will produce disturbances while achieving a real transformation in the social foundations of the theater. Carolina Civili (1869), the

Orrin brothers, who are destined to nourish the childhoods of several generations with fresh laughter, will come forth; the Teatro Arbeu will begin to be erected; Sofía Calderón, at the Principal, will perform in *The Obligations of a Home* (1874); Adelaida Ristori will shine in the *Medea* of Ernest Legouvé (December 31, 1874); the Spanish dramatic company of the actor Enrique Guasp de Peris (1875) will appear, and the Spanish Ristori, María Rodríguez, will arrive also (1876). It is an impressive list. Angela Peralta arises as gloriously as if she were a foreigner; Giacinta Pezzona de Gualtieri, along with *The Lady Innkeeper,* by Goldoni, *Hamlet, What Cannot be Said,* by Echegaray, and *Maximilian,* by her husband Luigi Gualtieri and which was coldly received, produces *Doña Leonora de Sarabia,* by Peón y Contreras, in Italian (1878); Leopoldo Burón appears, who later will discover Virginia Fábregas; the French opera company of Paola Marié brings with it a gamut of works which ranges from *Mignon* to *Madame Angot's Daughter,* including *Giroflé-Girofla,* by Lecoq; *The Clocktowers of Corneville; Madame Favart,* by Offenbach; *The Brigands; La Perichole; The Daughter of the Drum Major; The Little Duke; La Marjolaine,* and *Carmen,* by Bizet. The same year witnesses the inauguration of the Metropolitan Amphitheater of the Orrin brothers at the Seminario Plaza; The Ciutti Amphitheater of Pedro Servín, and the scintillations of Romualda Moriones in the *zarzuela.* 1882 receives the dramatic company of Adelaida Tessero; it hears *The Guaraní,* by Carlos Gómez, sung by La Peri and Francesco Giamini, and it suffers the pain of witnessing the death of Angela Peralta (August 30). Then the French opera company of Maurice Grau comes again as well as the English one of Hess, with Abbie Carrington and Emma Elsner (1883); Enrique Labrada devotes himself for almost thirty years to the *zarzuela,* and Napoleon Sieni arrives with his opera company (1885), and will return repeatedly, bringing *Falstaff, The Clowns, Manon Lescaut,* and *Mephistopheles,* by Boíto (1888)... The year 1886 salutes Ana Judic, and by the end of the year the hoax carried out by the false Marcus R. Mayer — Charles Bourdon —, the supposed agent of Adelina Patti, is exposed. But there is a real Mayer, and Miss Patti — in spite of everything — gives her first concert on December 15 at the Teatro Nacional, where she will return later, bringing with her

Francesco Tamagno (1890). In her rapid trip around the world Sarah Bernhardt touches Mexico and, after *The Lady of the Camellias,* "like La Civili, like La Ristori, like La Pezzana and La Rodríguez, she sees the theater almost empty, unlike the experience of many actors and actresses with much less talent than she" (1887).

There appear in 1887 *Juárez or The War of Mexico,* a drama by Gassier; the *zarzuela* company of Isidoro Pastor, in which Rosa Palacios, Enriqueta Alemany, Enriqueta Ors, Enriqueta Labrada and the Mexican José Vigil y Robles, also an author of *zarzuelas* like *The Metal-Founder* (1892); the pianist Voyer performs and in 1888 the dramatic company of Tomás Baladía appears in which there are beside himself Federico Alonso, María de Jesús Servín, Rita Cejudo, the comic actor Pedro Servín, and the character actor Felipe Montoya, both of whom are unforgettable for Mexico. In the same year there are the magician Kellar, the puppets of M. Gautier; and the opera of Antonini at the Arbeu; the swami Washington Irving Bishop, *Giaconda, Aída* and *Othello,* with Adela Gini Pizzorni and others, fill the stages. Still in that year, the puppets of Rosete Aranda are introduced and, for the first time, Luisa Martínez Casado, a Cuban reputed to be one of the loftiest figures of the dramatic art in the Spanish language who will return several times to Mexico, arrives. Coquelin, Sr., and Jane Hading appear in *The Ridiculous Précieuses;* Virginia Reiter and Giovanni Emanuel, in *Othello,* are presented in 1889. In the company of Leopoldo Burón, Antonio Contreras appears, with little success; the public is divided into supporters of Antonia Contreras and of Luisa Martínez Casado. Luis Roncoroni and Felicitá Prosdocimi with their dramatic company, the pianist Eugenio d'Albert; the pianist Berta Marx, said to be very beautiful, all arrive in 1890, a year which is remembered because of Pablo Sarasate.

The year 1891 stands out because of a hygienic measure taken in the theater: the dedication of theatrical functions or other public diversions to the authorities, functionaries or notables, is prohibited on pain of the payment of a fine of twenty to two hundred pesos. It is true that the former custom will be revived later, but something is gained in the meantime. Some theaters disappear: the Chamber of Deputies occupies the building of the Iturbide; the English opera company of Locke, with Emma Juch at its head, introduces operas by Richard Wagner (*Tannhauser, The Phantom Ship, The Walkyries*), by Weber (*Freischutz*), and by Beethoven (*Fidelio*) (1891). The void left by the departure of these brilliant items produces vertigo. While all of this was happening, *Chucho the Tramp* was being performed at the Teatro Arbeu; actors and actresses destined for the twentieth century were appearing: Elena Ureña (1890) and the "beautiful devotée" Virginia Fábregas.

However, "the principal theaters of the capital were devoted in shifts to the gracious, light and insubstantial *zarzuela*. The drama and the comedy, unsolicited by anyone and without artists capable of creating a demand for them, took refuge in the isolated Teatro Hidalgo." In the Orrin Amphitheater, Ricardo Bell seduces the multitude by doing the Kikirikí of *The Blue Testament* (1891).

It is maintained that between August 20, 1890 and May 15, 1892 twenty-three works were performed by Mexican authors, "of which nine met with extraordinary success, seven had a favorable reception, and three were hissed."

Nine Spanish and Mexican actors are outstanding: the Mexican tenor Felipe Reyes Retama, Ricardo López Ochoa, Ricardo Valero, son of José; Leopoldo Ortín, Victorial Sala, Carlota López de Leal... In Madrid the Mexican singer Antonia Ochoa de Miranda (1893) is brilliant. The children's troupe of Agustín Campuzano arises in 1894, the same year in which, to the general amusement of all, the aquatic farse entitled *A Wedding in Santa Lucía,* of French origin, is performed for the first time in the Orrin Amphitheater, and the black violinist Brindis de Salas is applauded.

On the occasion of the destruction of the stage of the Teatro Principal, because of the earthquake which occurred on All Saints' Day in the year 1894, the theater closes down after having remained open since 1753. The Teatro Nacional, for the same reason, suffered damage and is also closed after fifty years of operation. In 1895 a plan for a municipal theater is aborted; at the Nacional, now repaired, Antonio Vico and Antonia Contreras perform; the Cav. Andrea Maggi and Clara della Guardia, who was to perform by the side of Virginia Reiter, arrive simultaneously; the *zarzuela* troupe "The Breaking Dawn" performs at the Orrin Amphitheater; the children's troupe of Austri and Palacios, with several future stars, appears later, and there are operettas by Auber, by Audran and by Chapí, and guitarists such as Antonio Manjón. The opera company of the Russian Marie Tavary passes through; the Principal, repaired, is reopened; at the Arbeu, after the one of Guerra and Montoya, the dramatic company of Virginia Fábregas appears. Etelvina Rodríguez begins to appear in the *zarzuela* a little later...

On October 14, 1895, the first treaty concerning literary and artistic properties endorsed by Spain and Mexico takes effect, and in 1896 exhibitions of the Kinetoscope and of the Kinetophone of Edison are given for several months in the lower rooms of the house at Number 6, La Profesa Street, or Third Street in San Francisco. "The spectacle is beautiful and different, but it is too short for the price of fifty centavos per person charged by the management."

THE CONSERVATORY

THE OPERA EMPRESARIO BIACCHI, who came to Mexico with his company in 1865 and was favored by the Emperor Maximilian with a subsidy of four thousand pesos per month (which did not stop him from charging five thousand for a concert at the Palace), raised questions concerning the performance of the opera *Ildegonda* by Maestro Melesio Morales. The Emperor, who often protected the country's artists and had named Angela Peralta to be Privy Songstress and the leading actors at the Principal to be Performers of the Privy Chamber (all of whom were made to perform in the first part of *Don Juan Tenorio* in a specially constructed theater in the Palace), intervened in this matter. The necessary sum to calm the fears of the empresario concerning the success of the work having been sent, *Ildegonda* was sung shortly thereafter.

All of this, however, had its reflection directly in the public and, particularly, in a group of people who actively intervened so that the opera would be performed. As a result of this movement the founding body of the Philharmonic Society, a group which was later to become the present Conservatory of Music, was composed of those same persons. The relations which existed between the founders of the Philharmonic Society — Tomás León, Antonio García Cubas, Dr. José Ignacio Durán, Aniceto Ortega, Julio Ituarte and many others — and the literary figures of the Hidalgo Lyceum — Altamirano, Rosas Moreno, Guillermo Prieto, Manuel Flores, Ignacio Ramírez, Manuel Acuña, Justo Sierra, Francisco Pimentel, among the principal ones — resulted in the annexation of the Dramatic Conservatory, whose direction would have remained in the hands of the Spanish actor José Valero and his wife Salvadora Cairón if they had received the modest salary which they requested, by the Conservatory of Music.

The Lyceum of Mexico having been founded, on the other hand, through the initiative of José Tomás de Cuéllar, a dramatic section was included in it in which, among others, Amelia Estrella de Castillo, Donato Estrella and Gerardo López del Castillo figured. Great plans remained uncrystallized in this undertaking, among others an Agency for the Mexican Dramatic Gallery, which would have facilitated the publication of Mexican works.

Later, a small theater was constructed at the Conservatory with the funds obtained through a campaign headed by Antonio García Cubas which was carried out among the most distinguished members of Mexican society. This theater was opened on January 28, 1874 with great expectations.

In September, 1875, President Lerdo de Tejada granted the Conservatory a stipend of $4,800.00 pesos annually "to procure the advancement of the dramatic art in Mexico" which was given to the company of the Spanish actor Enrique Guasp de Peris, which was performing at the Teatro Principal, making incumbent upon it the obligation of giving preference to Mexican works. Thus on November 20 of that year *The Other Life,* by José Monroy, and later an adaptation of *The Dangerous Friends* by Ramón Manterola, which has been known since 1872, were performed. Along with these two works twelve foreign works are performed and *El Monitor* launches an attack on Guasp de Peris. In order to solve the difficulty, the Lyceum thought it appropriate to name a qualifying committee which would make decisions concerning the production of Mexican works, all of which drew another explosion from *El Monitor* on November 21: "The Recent Censorship: 'That Odious and Unconstitutional Institution Exists for Mexican Works.' Who is the Lyceum to set itself up as the public mentor? Who is the Lyceum to pretend that every author should be compelled to do something against his will?... The protection of the national literature be damned if the government subjects it to humiliation!"

As a result of these attacks numerous Mexican works were performed in the year 1876 — a unique year. Among them the following may be mentioned: *The Maurels,* by Roberto Esteva; *As High as the Sky,* by José Peón y Contreras; *The Daily Bread,* by José Rosas Moreno; *The Sacrifice of Life, Gil González de Avela, The King's Daughter, A Love Affair of Hernán Cortés,*

Struggles of Honor and Love, Juan de Villalpando, Impulses of the Heart and *Antón de Alaminos,* all by Peón y Contreras; *María,* by Alberto Biancho; *The Adulterous Man* by Esteva; *Ambition and Coquetry,* by J. Sebastián Segura; *Churubusco,* by José Monroy; *Sor Juana Inés de la Cruz,* by Rosas Moreno; *A Lily Among the Brambles,* by Isabel Prieto de Landázuri, who died in Hamburg on September 28 of that year; *The Mexican Conspiracy,* by Gustavo Baz; *María,* by Obregón; *Love is Repaid with Love,* by José Martí; *The Box of Candy,* by Rafael Delgado, and *The Slave,* by Rafael de Zayas Enríquez.

It should not be forgotten that in the performance of *The King's Daughter,* by José Peón y Contreras, the playwright spent a terribly unpleasant moment when he was presented the crown and the golden plume in a disastrous ceremony.

This period having passed, Mexican works continued to be produced, although in a much smaller proportion, with Mexican and foreign actors such as Merced Morales, Manuel Estrada, Gerardo López del Castillo, Concha Méndez, Concha Padilla, Valero and his wife and Giacinta Pezzana. These works were "imitative theater, theater with no soul or body, and they normally were not even clad, by way of compensation, in the trappings of form... After 1890 scarcely a play or two by a Mexican author appears. As always, works written abroad rule the stage."

The fall of President Lerdo de Tejada brought to an end the awarding of the stipend to the Conservatory, and the reprisals taken by persons in the government which succeeded him — according to the historians — meant an end to the Conservatory's theater and caused instruction in the dramatic art to stagnate there. Furthermore, the nine month period during which Enrique Guasp de Peris enjoyed that subsidy — which was not always paid on time — did not produce brilliant results with regard to the theatrical education of the students either.

FRONTIER

THE TWENTIETH CENTURY in the theater has its true origin in Virginia Fábregas. However from the time at which she began to act, at the side of the Spanish actor Leopoldo Burón in the last decade of the nineteenth century, there is nothing in her of the odious fin-de-siècle condition. She is the first actresss with vision, not of what the theater was then but of what it would be later, and consequently she is the first modern actress in Mexico.

Like Angela Peralta, like Antonia Ochoa de Miranda, she marks a break with the habit, and it was certainly a bad one, which had been requiring up until that time a traditional role. She has no other physical handicap than that of language, no other spiritual limitation than the one placed upon her by the genre which she has chosen. Before her there were no specialists.

If she offers a pristine tribute to the pure Spanish theater, the Spanish stage does not attract her nor stagnate her with its farcical traits, and she constitutes the first national example of one who does not live from the theater but for the theater.

The French works which had occupied in Mexico a place proportionally similar to that of the Mexican theater are the ones which point out for her the modern path which our literatures will follow together with — in caricature — several years of our social life. It is she who makes the French theater with all its merit and all of its defects necessary for the public, and France paid a national debt when it awarded her the Academic Palms in 1908. She has goals, and does not delay her apprenticeship. With her the public does not sit in contemplation of useless and vain things, and those who attended the theater at that time discovered, thanks to her, a new theatrical continent: education. Virginia Fábregas, not satisfied merely with educating, learned as well.

XVII. Virginia Fábregas

Courtesy of Miss Virginia Fábregas

Her life, fortunately a long one devoted entirely to the theater, shows her to be always at a consistent level of harmony and devotion. Those who saw her when she was a young woman, enlivening the theater of Victoriano Sardou, recall the sumptuous propriety of her wardrobe, the decorative scenery, the correctness in staging, the artistic pulchritude to which she has always aspired in her labor of dignification. If that paraphernalia had the defect of being, like all the trappings of its times, less elegant than what was believed, it had on the other hand the merit of not having ever been seen in Mexico previously. "Thanks to her, we have been introduced in the course of a decade to the most successful works on European stages, done with the same luxuriousness, but with good taste, which was previously unknown on our stages where the sets, the backdrop, the refinement in production were, all in all, a bit less than unknown. Donnay, Capus, Hervieu, Lavedan (Brieux, Hermant), Benavente, the Alvarez Quinteros, the best of the French and Spanish repertories, have paraded through the theaters wherever Virginia Fábregas appeared."

The theatrical production of Mexico was not generally at her level; but all that was most consistent and most profound was worthy of her attention: from *The King's Daughter,* by José Peón y Contreras, to the theater of Marcelino Dávalos, passing through *The Serf's Revenge,* by Federico Gamboa, which she directed.

Far from enveloping herself in the attitude of serving the public by giving to it only that which is impressive, Virginia Fábregas seeks everything, sees everything; she travels carrying with her our most illustrious embassy of the genre to all the Spanish-speaking countries.

She is remembered in the glow of *Madame Mistress* and of *Lady X,* and with the fresh grace of *Madame Sans-Gêne.*

Now she turns toward Eugene O'Neill and Pirandello with indefatigable enthusiasm. She alone possesses the energy, the refinement and the knowledge. Her talent has abided with her harmoniously and contiguously. Virginia Fábregas, respecting the public and herself, is the theatrical exception who has not trampled the memory of her youthful creations among the audience.

In Mexico she alone constitutes a theatrical allegory.

RETURN TRIP

The Authors

THROUGHOUT THIS INVESTIGATIVE WORK, which is frequently wearisome but which had the merit of heightening my scepticism toward historical material, I have found one pervasive phenomenon: the difficulty of making a critical evaluation. With the exception of the autoctonous theater and the religious theater, theatrical movements in Mexico are characterized by a lack of trends and a dearth of finalities. There are individuals, but there is no theatrical society. No one follows the lead of Juan Ruiz de Alarcón, whose status as a Mexicanist is sufficient to create a Mexican school; no one follows Juana Inés de la Cruz in neatness of procedure; no one follows the lead of Manuel Eduardo de Gorostiza or, in the final analysis, of the foreign authors who from the nineteenth century onward stoke the aging fires of our stages. The writers of magical plays and *sainetes,* of works with carnival contours and of types destined to relieve, with a delicacy which was as equivocal as it was vain, the spectators of their money, are revived and imitated. The absence of great innovators is not symptomatic, for they came after the combined and conscious effort of the great artesans. There are no great theatrical toilers with the exception of José Peón y Contreras. Similarly, the Romantic movement aside — which culminated in the developed countries thanks to *Werther* and The Rights of Man — and which was a uniform if not genial movement here, among all the rest of the authors the lack of a school is more than obvious.

The theater is a passion in itself; an attraction in its primitive form. However in the scant theatrical society of Mexico the authors seem to embark on a purposeless venture, with the vague idea of putting their talent to the test — or the opposite — in that genre as well. The attraction does not become a passion; the passion is almost never perfected in them, and does not even seem to excite them to complete possession. The fickleness previously pointed out in a majority of writers converts them into a type of eligible bachelors of the theater: they send a bouquet of flowers to the comedy, a bottle of perfume to the tragedy, a box of bonbons to the *zarzuela* and some silk stockings to the revue. But no betrothals ensue. The theater, because of the fact that they give up nothing of themselves, is used like a forbidden way of life in a kind of provisional adultery. Why? the theater is as honorable as any other art and is as worthy of that divorceless marriage that lyric poetry, painting and music enjoy. Because of the bourgeois simile they are nuptials between a man and art, they are unique, and are like the man and horse which are united in the centaur. In these five to seven multiples — as the French would say — of the theater in Mexico, when someone had written a costumbrist play he immediately felt the unrestrained desire to do the libretto for a *zarzuela* without concerning himself further with the drama. There is something between the profane and painful interior of the bare theater and the tinselled gaudiness of its paper decorations. No one grasps it. The theater sees itself alienated from its real goal by the froth of modern Spanish production which, if one can say it, is characterized by the lack of characters; it is a theater of stucco and often of cardboard in which there is no criticism of customs or of psychology, philosophy, or even fantasy as a laboratory for an imaginary life; it is a theater without a past or a future, always of a certain moment and never of a particular moment. Furthermore, if the last Romantic gasp of the theater in the nineteenth century seems to be more compact and a little more respectful of itself — in certain cases — it is consequently no less overdue or foreign to the new modulation of the artistic idea and alien to the social morality which follows. In it, as in all the previous movements, there is a period of relapse, of stagnation, of immobility. This happens because the previous problem in each case has not been solved or even understood at times, and persists. A renovation of the activity, in this sense as in others of the five national senses, is equivalent to a patient's awakening to find his illness beside him; to a lazy laborer's opening his eyes after not finishing his nap and having to devote the new day to his old job. In addition, the Mexican mentality, which is teratological if we wish to cling to Mr. Freud's anecdote, contributes to this because it does not evolve or proceed ostensibly to higher planes. It is a great mentality, doubtlessly; but the fertilizing qualities of manure are negative in art. Art takes in small bits and gives in great quantities and, furthermore, the base humor of so many writers from past centuries is not quite as primitive a form of intellect as ours.

On the other hand, while the detestable end-of-the-century taste — French on this occasion (see *1900,* by Paul Morand) — takes possession of architecture and the great lesser arts such as fashion and jewelry, between the inexpressive muteness and the mute expression of the theater in Mexico there arises a fundamental problem which is not grasped, of course, by the humble hands of our dramaturgy: the problem of social evolution.

If art still rules half the terrain in Europe — an art of decadent culminations — social uneasiness rules the other half. Still far from the masses, a metal assayed only by experts, the transformation is in the hands of the intellectuals. Russia occupies in it all its thinkers, all its novelists, all its essayists, all its short story writers, which is without parallel except for Maupassant, its lyric and dramatic poets from the middle of the nineteenth century onward. The voice of Karl Marx is raised in Germany; France, always receptive to psychological speculations, the fairy godmothers of Nietzsche, does not obstruct this work; in England, George Bernard Shaw, beginning in the eighties, gathers himself unto himself. But Mexico suffers in this regard from the backwardness of Spain in a prolongation of the colonial hegemony, a fatal comet with a long tail. In that peace, after the manner of Octavian, of the first ten years of the century, lyric poetry flourishes in decadence; importation increases; journalism is modernized; communications enjoy an early round of success. People write, and the writing is beautiful. People write beautifully following the Wildean maxim of the inutility of art, which was falsified in spite of its fine spirit because it was utilized. There are forces which are available; but either the censorship is extreme or there are no authors capable of grasping the new life which is forming in the atmosphere. According to the statements of some contemporaries that is the first thing which occurs; according to others it is the second. It is, then, both things. In the face of the emptiness of the exquisite forms of that time —there is no vulgarity in the adjective— which were wasted on journalism, I have reached the point of asking myself if none of those men who heard the voice of foreign influences wrote a diary with ulterior motives which would be published upon his death and enlighten the following generation concerning the occult currents of thought; if none said of the era any of the things which Talleyrand said of Napoleon; if no one, in short, had foresight. I consider that the intensity of the social problem was still less; that Mexico was not, consciously at least, in the same condition as Russia, notwithstanding the fact that it offered a synonymous problem of east and west, of old things and new things. At any rate, I am unaware of any similar Lenin in the theater or even of any analogous Victor Hugo or Ignacio Ramírez. Did Díaz Mirón foresee anything? Yes, certainly. But in the first place — and it is necessary to thank him for it — he was an artist, and he had the right to believe that there is no doctrine possible with hiatuses, alliterations, redundancies or verbage. And, furthermore, he wrote nothing for the theater. Nevertheless, it can be stated that the imposing Leo Tolstoy set frontiers aside. Emilio Rabasa seasoned his novels with spices which are still in use today. Small groups of malcontents caused disturbances on the street corners which were symbolic of the larger social street corner on which the country found itself. But beside the fact — as a contemporary informs me — that peace after the manner of... was like a rainbow following the many downpours of the now defunct century, progress was made by elimination and by abstraction. The insignificant were eliminated and the great were attracted, after their initial concern, to their "hunger and thirst for justice" and thrust into another realm of ideas. These were things which, in short, if they excused the social silence would not excuse the theatrical silence. For if there was no prophetic or revolutionary production, neither was there simply an artistic one.

The libretto of the *zarzuela Consuelo*, written by Amado Nervo — with music by Antonio Cuyás —, was entertaining. A *Quo Vadis,* said to be unforgettable, with a libretto by Alberto Michel, is performed in 1902 at the Teatro Renacimiento, which was later the Teatro Virginia Fábregas, which was afterwards the Teatro Mexicano and later — I hope for good — the Teatro Virginia Fábregas. On the same stage in 1905 *The Serf's Revenge,* by Federico Gamboa, is presented. If Virginia Fábregas is successful in performing it with

her unaided nationalistic bent, the play, whose title would be pro-
mising if it did not mention "serf," does not involve a social conflict
other than in its Romantic matrix of the differences between castes,
or a problem of interests, except with regard to the personal interests
in conflict. There is not even a question of society in it, yet it does
deal with people. If the anachronisms paraded on the stage are
classical ones, the motive which propels them is not yet a motor
capable of inflaming and setting the audience in motion. It is drama,
of course, and therefore explains the uniqueness of Federico Gamboa in the genre, which is manifest and may enhance his merit as
an artesan. Another lonely voice is heard in the provinces: *The
Last Chapter,* by Manuel José Othón, is performed in the same year
in San Luis Potosí. At this stage, which would be appropriate for
the sixteenth century, we find in the following year a *Cuauhtémoc,*
by Tomás Domínguez Illanes, which is also performed at the
Teatro Renacimiento by Virginia Fábregas and her company.
The public administration of the time may be said to have done
what it could in stimulating the theater: in the drama contest
sponsored by the Secretariat of Public Instruction and Fine Arts
in 1906, the drama *Head and Heart,* written by Teresa Farías de
Isasi, wins the prize. Virginia Fábregas stages *Thus They Pass,* by
Marcelino Dávalos, in 1908, a work which foreshadows nothing in
this epoch of blind peace in spite of its nationalistic character, and
Judgment Day, by José Joaquín Gamboa. In 1909, Tina di Lorenzo
produces *The Strongest Woman,* a work by a certain García Fi-
gueroa, and Virginia Fábregas performs in *Tragic Gardens* and
Marciano's Crime, by Marcelino Dávalos. Another new author appears in 1910: Antonio Mediz Bolio, who produces *Mountain
Winds* and *The Executioner,* and to increase the number one must
count the Catalan José Escofet who writes and has produced here
The Tragedy of the Roses. If it is remembered that in this same
first decade French was an inevitable language for intellectuals in
Mexico; that the magazine *L'Illustration* had been publishing in its
supplements the theatrical works performed in France since the
previous century, and that these included the plays of Paul Bourget
which described the social movement; that King Alfonso XIII and
Queen Victoria had been on the verge of being murdered during
an anarchist assasination attempt on the very day of their wedding;

all of that, along with several other similar things, will complete the description of the inexplicable theatrical silence in Mexico.

More fortunate, the opera produces *Atzimba,* by Ricardo Castro, with libretto by Alberto Michel (1900); *The Poet King,* by Gustavo Campa and Alberto Michel, which achieves the distinction of being sung in Milan (1900); *Zulema,* by Ernesto Elorduy, with libretto by Rubén M. Campos (1903); *The Legend of Rudel,* by Ricardo Castro, concerning the pleasant theme of the troubadour of Aquitaine, sung by the company of Aldo Barilli (1906), and *Nicholas Bravo,* by Rafael J. Tello, with a libretto based on an adaptation of the drama by Ignacio Mariscal (1910). In addition, *Satan Vanquished* and *La Roussalska,* unpublished operas by Ricardo Castro, who died in 1907, should be counted. The national *zarzuela,* which will become a large-scale enemy of the drama, is not lacking in glory: there is *The Lady Sergeant,* with libretto by Aurelio González Carrasco and music by Rafael Gascón (1903); *Chin-Chun-Chan,* by Rafael Medina and José F. Elizondo with music by Luis G. Jordá, which reaches one hundred performances at the Teatro Principal (1904), and in which figure personalities who will fill the lesser stages for years to come such as María Luisa Labal, Paco Gavilanes, Consuelo Vivanco, Eduardo Arozamena, Esperanza Iris... On the other hand, the demolition of the old Teatro Nacional is carried out in 1901 in order to widen the Avenida Cinco de Mayo, at the end of which the cornerstone of the new Teatro Nacional, whose construction takes on dictatorial proportions, is laid. The newspapers of the time comment on the event calling it "destruction for construction," and it is in this way that one of the most productive mechanisms for jokes in the country comes into being.

Suddenly...

At one hundred year's distance from the first basic revolution a second equally basic one leaves its great mark on the history of Mexico at that time, bringing to the surface problems which had been dormant since the medieval colonial period. It is a revolution which apparently derives from casual laws or from biological accumulations because it is a surprise from its beginning to its accomplishment and because it leaves everything behind in such a way that it converts all men into temporary employees whether they are for it or against it. It is a revolution of military and political antecedents, to be sure; but it is not one of theatrical or intellectual antecedents, which would be impossible for the ideal archtype of a *Green Cockatoo* and without harbingers in the style of a Tolstoy, of a Kuprin, of a Gorky, or of a Kropotkine. It is a secular and vertiginous action which precedes the way of thinking which it is preparing and the thought which understands like a blow to the face that in the fist not just thirty years of peace but four centuries of cobwebs and subjection are lurking.

Then comes the race which exhausts the endurance of the men, who, incapable of thinking, feel that to remain behind means to miss forever the great train of change and of re-evaluations and remain forgotten in the desert.

Although it is surely unknown, because of a common phenomenon in the world of thought, the genially equivocal maxim of Goethe which anticipates the works of circumstances is a label placed on all new actions. At the moment works are made for the moment. The intellectual revolution begins with the third act. Thus *The Old* by Marcelino Dávalos appears (1911). Thus the latitudinal motives of the revolution, which at times will appear to be unfathomable and endless.

Another hour strikes for the theater in Mexico. The theme is immense, the time is short. Does the theater want a voice, "a voice to shout with"? At the Arbeu there appear *The Goat's Foot, The Devil's Auction, Mother Celestina's Magic Powders*; at the Fábregas, *The Law of Karma,* by a certain Dr. Krumm Heller, a German living in Mexico. Is this the time to create a new theater? *The Maderista Tenorio* and, more importantly, *The Furrow,* by José F. Elizondo and J. Rafael Rubio with music by the composers Gascón and Uranga, appear. With the exception of Marcelino Dávalos, in the work cited no one answers the call of the dramatic theater. This is the opportune time for the triumph of the lesser genres which are, as such, the slaves of opportunism. From this emanates the secret of the future of the theater. The *zarzuela,* restricted little by little in Spanish productions, gives over a part of its extensive terrain to the revue, a succession of events connected by the single thread of a passer-by or tourist which will create generic types like the girl who sells lottery tickets and the drunk girl, the grotesque foreigner, the pear-shaped political candidate, the policeman, the stool-pigeon, the half-breed, the bumpkin who has come to the city, the pickpocket, the talkative barber, etc. National problems, which

are pressing, current conflicts, the political atmosphere, are often
commented upon in those scenes with obscene witticisms, with vulgar
music. But the blame must be placed on the non-existent playwrights. All of this gives to the revue the rights to the introduction
of the theater into this century.

On an involuntary road to perfection, this genre turns to new
resources, it unfolds collections of regional costumes, cultivates
typical music, refines their representative characters and, even if it
encourages an unfathomable mediocrity with regard to works, it is
able to produce its own authors and, more importantly, its own
actors, such as Leopoldo Beristáin and Lupe Rivas Cacho at first,
and later Roberto Soto. The two men mark the two stages of the
revue. Over a period of twenty years the genre sustains itself on
anything it can find, always alive and permanent, always in tune
with life as it unfolds, filled with an inner warmth which is not
perfect, of course, but which exists; which is neither spirit nor
flame, but which is tepidity. Through the revue pass songs from the
south, from the north and from the lowlands, captured in the expe-
ditions which these correspondents of the theater make to the inte-
riors of the books on folk-lore, and sometimes to the interior of the
Republic; lacquers, costumes from Michoacán and Oaxaca, half-
breed girls from Yucatán, girls from Tehuantepec, cowboys from
Tamaulipas, sarapes from Saltillo, songs and dances from the four
Huastec provinces and from the State of Mexico, dances like the
huapungo, jarabe and *sandunga,* all of which are frequently adul-
terated, are concocted and stylized: but, in short, they are exhibited.
And the works, particularly the ones produced in the early periods,
often go beyond one hundred performances. It is true that their
evolution is slow and that they bear the weight of obscenity in the
main; that it is frequently some kind of torrid animalistic theater
which could be more clearly defined as the national theater of sex;
that the authors and actors in numerous cases enclose themselves in
a circle of torpidity and lasciviousness without the spirit to explore
the other eight spheres of art; that behind the picturesque curtain
there lurks an aphrodisiacal backdrop and behind the proverbial and
nationalistic expression is lodged the monstrous epithet or the purely
bestial play on words. It is true that there is often ugliness and
almost always too fragile a beauty in this theater; that there are
not any *Adventures of King Pausole* or a *Lysistrata,* even with a

Maurice Donnay in it; that there are plagiarisms, imitations, parodies, particularly parodies, all this plus inertia and retardation of its
own personality, good moments stolen from a more original wit and
— shall I say kleptomania? — which are common to a great number
of authors. It is true that in this theater almost everything dies by
itself and in itself, that it is a regression, one of the things left
undone in the centuries of gestation already past; but there is in it,
however rudimentarily, an organized if not refined life which is, if
not ascendant, continuous.

Apart from the authors already mentioned, Carlos Ortega, Pablo
Prida, Juan D. del Moral and Sandoval deserve mention for the
most intense and constant toil, and among the musicians the same
applies to José Palacios and Manuel Castro Padilla.

The bare and coarse period excites the chroniclers: "Fortunately,
it seems that Grazi and Beristáin alone will vie with each other for
the prize for immorality." (Luis de Larroder, *El Mundo Ilustrado,*
1914.) Among the *zarzuelas The Lady Sergeant,* which has already
been mentioned, and *At the Hacienda,* by Federico Carlos Keggel,
are judged to be acceptable; but "there are mountains of them
which are an eternal shame, a real outrage to morality, to literature,
to the dramatic art." (Ricardo del Castillo, *Revista de Revis-
tas,* 1915.)

Criticism experiences, on the other hand, a meager and deficient
life. It hides timidly behind simple narration, which is sometimes
gallant, sometimes ugly, and is of Spanish extraction. The habit of
narrating plots prevails which is useless for those who have seen
a play and unpleasant for those who have not yet seen it. There
is no artistic analysis, nor is criticism treated as an art. All sacrifices
are made on the altars of friendship for the writers or for their
position, for the benefit of the newspapers and for their advertising
budgets. Or, rather, personal passions are satisfied in the columns
of criticism: revenge for cancelled passes, refusals of seats or of
the pleasant favors of the actresses. But there is something more
important which is neglected: the creative function. In criticism
progress is not made through praise or condemnation. Applause is
an item of the code of good conduct of the audience and it has no
creative value. It is often a gift of bad taste, and implies only a
superficial or social enthusiasm when it explodes after the last work
of a clever "To be or not to be"; or it is an impertinent demand

that Hamlet cease being Hamlet in order to once again become a
vain and servile actor. To applaud after the last note of the Fifth
Symphony, or after the last step of Ana Pavlova, is an attempt on
the life of art and the sacrifice of an inner emotion for an epidermal
and nervous sensation. It means that the audience has not been
carried away from itself or from its conventions by the strength
of the performer, or that it has not been capable of grasping it, that
it is lacking in sensitivity since, without any transition, it passes
from the planet of Art to the planet Earth, and that on leaving the
theater it will forget what it has seen or heard. Applause, truly, is
typical of the multitude, and enthusiasm has a physical implication
as well; but in all these examples applause is as lowly as man's
laughter.

In criticism progress is made — suppose this supposition — by
stating whether a work of art has been done with an awareness of
the great rules or whether they have been ignored; whether its
artistic condition is not falsified by its human condition and whether
or not the latter has violated the limits of art. Progress is made
by teaching the members of the audience to discern the solidity of
art just as, in the schools, they are taught how to read and write:
the basics of artistic orthography are placed in their hands so that
they may utilize it and may judge whether the work which is presented to them has spelling errors in it or not. Progress is made by
teaching the audience to flee from that which is false in art just
as children are taught to avoid a nasty expression or sloppy diction,
seeing an unpleasant sight or hearing the conversation of drunks.
Progress is made in criticism by guiding the actor and the author
toward the antecedents of their art, something of which they are
frequently unaware. Criticism neither applauds nor curses: affirms
nor denies. It is disdainful if the coarseness of the work does not
raise itself to its level. Criticism is, in reality, the eighth art even
though it may not be, unfortunately, all that Oscar Wilde desires.
Here the same thing has occurred to criticism which has happened
to the theater: experiments are tried, attempts are made; rarely are
satisfactory results obtained. After the well-liked chroniclers, who
did not possess pure critical faculties such as those of the first
illustrated magazines of the century, others survive who, in many
instances, lack the philosophical and literary training of the former.
Dragged along by a vocation with no restraints, a vocation similar

to that of a leaf on a vine, they carry out the willful task of misguiding the public. It has been maintained on numerous occasions that if there are no critics in Mexico it is because no literary society in a state of productivity exists. If this is true it does not justify the absence of critics. The critic is not a neighborhood barber, and the artistic work of the entire world offers itself to the critics of the whole world. The foreign theatrical works presented in Mexico had no legal status of any sort. Inferior in the main, they demonstrated when they were imposed that in reality there were no critics capable of vanquishing them in front of the audience.

The truth is that the revolution is prolonged, and that the *género chico* progresses and infects the indiscriminate taste of the spectators.

A three act poem by José Santos Chocano, "The Conquistadores" (1912); adaptations of *The Serf's Revenge* and *Mountain Winds,* together with *Light and Shadow,* by Farías de Isasi (I am told that a history should contain everything); *Part Payment,* by Federico Gamboa; *The Mexican Revolution,* by Ladislao López Negrete; *To Caesar...,* by the soprano and actress Mimí Derba; *Ad Majorem Dei Gloriam,* by Alberto Michel; *The Last Picture,* by Marcelino Dávalos; *A Feat,* by Rafael Pérez Taylor; *Eagles and Stars,* a "dramatic film" by Marcelino Dávalos; *Victim of His Guilt,* a three act drama in verse by Luis Castro y López; *The Broken Puppet,* by Manuela Eugenia Torres, also the author of *Conquered* and *Around the Chimera*; all these works are part of the passing scene. At about the same time (1916-1917), at the Teatro Ideal *A Doll's House* (called *A Doll's Home* by Carlos Barrera who translated it from the Norwegian) is staged, and the charge for admission is eight centavos in national currency. Afterwards comes *Indissoluble,* by Marcelino Dávalos; new authors begin to appear such as Julio Jiménez Rueda (*Christmas Ballad*), María Luisa Ross (*Roses of Love*), and Arnulfo Miramontes, opera *Anáhuac* is performed with a libretto by a certain Bracho (1918). In Yucatán, on the other hand, in the year 1918 alone, works are performed by Arturo Peón Cisneros (*The Foam*); by Ermilo Abreu Gómez (*In the Mountains*); by Horacio Villamil (*Moonlit Night*); by Mimenza y Hernández (*The Bells*); by Antonio Mediz Bolio (*The Wave,* which is also produced in Mexico City that same year); and by Delio Moreno Cantón along with *The King's Daughter,* by José Peón y Contreras, which is revived.

The Arrow of The Sun, by Mediz Bolio, and *The Way to Perfection,* by Julio Jiménez Rueda — then the director of the School of Theatrical Arts (1918), and whose work *As in Real Life* is given a prize in the contest sponsored by the University to celebrate the anniversary of Independence — are added to this store. *The Guilty One,* by Manuela Eugenia Torres; *Spirit,* by Pérez Taylor, can also be mentioned during this same period. Prolific writers are not lacking — how could they be? —. The presbyter Atenógenes Segale, I am told, composes tragedies in verse in torrential fashion in a single night such as *The Royal Purple, Diocletian, The Dioscuri* and a hundred more which receive awards from the local schools.

With regard to the minor genres, they are enriched — and not simply metaphorically — with works such as *The Land of the Machine Gun,* by Elizondo and Gascón; *The Nation's Muses,* by Elizondo and Xavier Navarro, known only through *The Ashen Duck*; *The Military Academy,* by Miguel Wimer — who was for many years an actor and stage director in operettas, *zarzuelas,* and revues — and the "veteran" Capella; *At The Hacienda*; *The City of the Trucks*; *On the War Front*; *The Land of the Volcanoes,* by Ortega y Castro; *Chaplin The Candidate,* by Guz Aguila; and, in spite of the prohibition by the department of the District Government regarding the treatment of political matters on the stage, there are *Don Adolfo's Orchard,* by Guz Aguila and José Palacios, and *Sister Water,* by Tirso Sáenz, Alberto Michel and Vigil, which was censured by the municipal government (1920); *National Bargain Sale,* by Wimer and Palacios; *The Very Honorable Municipal Government* and *Obregón's Garden,* by Ortega, Prida and Castro Padilla, all of whom also wrote *National Currents* (1921).

Rafael M. Saavedra, the author of *The Crossing* and other works, founded in December, 1921, after the erection of the open air theater at San Juan Teotihuacán, what would later be organized with the name Mexican Regional Theater under the sponsorship of the Secretariat of Public Education. After the religious theater, this is the first systematized movement known, in spite of the existence from previous times of the Regional Theater of Yucatán, since the latter had been operating principally because of tradition.

At the present time open air theaters exist in practically all the cities and towns of the Republic. They are theaters constructed by the Indians themselves under the supervision of rural schoolteachers,

and in them, besides plays for entertainment, works of anti-alco-
holic and moral propaganda are performed which are messengers
inspired by the benefits of the revolutions and the need for work
and love among the peasants. Also in this instance, apart from
works with themes controlled for educational purposes, the Indians
are encouraged not only to perfom but to compose plays in their
own languages as well as in Spanish, for which contests are sponsored, and it is maintained that the enthusiasm which they pour
into them is equal only to that displayed by their ancestors at the
time of the development of the religious theater. They cultivate,
as they did previously, their artistic, rhythmic and symbolic senses.
They paint, moreover, by themselves the masks necessary for the
presentations of their traditional dances: "The Clay Pots,"
"The Little Indians," "The Old Men," from the State of Michoacán, and "The Goldminers," from Guerrero, and for those of
more recent invention such as "Industrious Zacualtipán" and "The
Cane Cutters," from the State of Morelos. The next to the last,
which is written by the musician Jesús Gaona, is a choreographic
representation of the native industries, a rhythmic pantomine of
the daily labors of leatherworking and iron working. The last is
a description of the enslavement and labor of the Indians of the
State of Morelos on the sugar cane plantations. Rafael M. Saavedra has given me the following description of this latter spectacle:
"Dressed in humble clothing, which is in rags; with their faces
covered with grime, exhausted, a little drunk, the cane cutters go
out to work accompanied by their wives led by the foreman who,
with his pistol by his side and his whip in his hand, watches over
and flogs them while threatening to dock their salaries if they do
not put forth greater effort. Afterwards a series of events occurs
which is filled with color and great plastic effort interpreting the
facets of work done on the plantation up to the moment when
the foreman adorns himself with a crown and takes in his arms a
doll fashioned of corn meal — which symbolizes food — and presents it to the dancers who fall to their knees around him."

This process of classical extraction which, according to my
information, gives satisfactory results generally, has within itself
room for one danger at least. In the sixteenth century the theater
had not yet entirely gotten away from religious themes. The methods
must not have been greatly different. In Mexico City, just as in

Cholula and Tlaxcala, in Yucatán as well as in Veracruz, and everywhere outside the country, the theater was about the same age and only offered that variety constituted by different dialects and languages. In the twentieth century the essential varieties persist — they are basic — but the methods are multiplied by diversity, particularly through competition with the cinematographer. The world becomes smaller, also, as the first man and later the machine grow in number. Truth, on the other hand, in order to appear truthful — it has lost its appearance to many would-be truths — needs to be uniform. A man educated by a purely regional theater, required by it to improve on local customs, and the possessor by means of it of one truth, perhaps will not be able to maintain his equilibrium when he sees himself suddenly thrust into another theater which is representative of other customs and of another truth which is contemporary to them and completely opposed to them. This situation produces people who are referred to as unadaptable. All of us learn to walk in walkers or led by the hands of adults. But we would never learn to walk if we did not see others walk. My theory is that the intelligence of the Indians, confined within a theater of their own which is not aware of other theaters, cannot be directed toward other than a local manifestation, and that the phenomenon of disunion is produced so long as no absolute rhythm dominates the social and theatrical procedures of a nation. Not in ten years or in twenty or in more can the domination of an art form which has gone through a process of centuries of evolution be acquired. I fear that if it is not forced, the process will ultimately be, if not negative because the theater is opposed to that condition, at least deficient and incomplete. It would be necessary to determine up to what point this system encourages the independence of the Indian as an Indian, and to what degree it attempts to incorporate the new ethnic ideal and make of it a domain, or at least a pathway, for the new Mexican. This is not a rationale for the elimination of that educational method or for the abolition of tradition. It mitigates, at the most, in favor of the modern tendency to play down the innate differences between men, and to lighten their burden of traditions to such a degree as not to impede their progress, because of their weight, or to make of them, were they to be lightened too much, slaves to the winds.

After all, the cosmic race is nearer now than what we ourselves believe.

In the year 1922 there is an effort to establish a Mexican theater: in the theater called the Comedia (Lírico), works by Marcelino Dávalos (*Thus They Pass, Tragic Gardens*), by Teresa Farías de Isasi (*Religion of Love*), by Guz Aguila (*Blood on the Jaripeo*), by Rafael M. Saavedra (*Check the King*), and by Armando de María y Campos, whose play is, in fact, *The Last Rose* of the Teatro de la Comedia, although it belonged to him only partly, are staged.

In reality it is in the year 1923 when the most important movements in the theater in Mexico are begun, movements which in spite of the intervals which separate them, because of the presence in almost all of them of the same people, are the equivalent to a similar prolonged effort during the subsequent ten year period. In the first place is the return to Mexico of the actress María Teresa Montoya, which brings to the stage works by Julio Jiménez Rueda, by Ricardo Parada León and by Catalina d'Erzell. The first mentioned divides his theatrical activity between one tendency toward local color and another toward historical theater. The second is perhaps the most praiseworthy seeker of the human element on the national stage. Elsewhere, Ricardo Mutio and Prudencia Grifell perform a work by José Joaquín Gamboa: *The Devil is Cold*.

Scarcely is he promoted to the dignified position of Secretary of the Municipal Council of Mexico City, when Julio Jiménez Rueda employs his influence immediately in favor of the theater and, because of his efforts on May 25, 1923, that entity requests the dramatic troupes of the capital to form a Municipal Theater. The subsidy, which is $3,500.00 pesos per month, is awarded to the company of María Teresa Montoya, who on the following twenty-third of June opens her season at the Teatro Virginia Fábregas. During the period when she appears there only five Mexican works are staged: *The Fall of The Flowers,* by Julio Jiménez Rueda; *Things of Life* by María Luisa Ocampo; *Suitor Number Thirteen,* by Alberto Michel; *Up to date,* by Federico Sodi, and for the benefit of María Teresa Montoya in November of the same year, *Sister Adoration of the Divine Word,* by Julio Jiménez Rueda. This movement which has no precedent in this century naturally sets all the authors and chroniclers to work. When the city government establishes a committee to approve plays, composed of Federico Gamboa, Ramón Riveroll and Eduardo Colín, the press screams about the prior censorship in 1875; there are attacks of all types and even controversies. In the meanwhile, María Teresa Montoya alternates foreign works with Mexican works, (*Zazá, Don Juan's Madness*) and, finally, the Municipal Theater concludes with the previously mentioned benefit.

However, the first step having been taken — not without pecuniary motivations — there is an immediate result; while the Teatro Municipal functions, the publicity which the Mexican authors suddenly acquire justifies their presence on other stages. Mercedes Navarro performs in *The Woman Who Came Back to Life,* by María Tubau and Francisco Monterde, the author of *In The Whirlpool* which was produced earlier at the Teatro Colón, and *Chanito,* by Catalina Erzell. A second result is produced a short while later: the authors begin to organize themselves, and the formation of the UDAD (Unión de Autores Dramáticos) dates from the same year, 1923. The founders were: Julio Jiménez Rueda, Francisco Monterde, María Montes, Ricardo Parada León, Rafael M. Saavedra and Eugenia Torres. This is all that is achieved, and it is not insignificant if one takes into account the fact that in reality it is the first thing of this sort done.

Something else is begun: the "Mexican Evenings of Theatrical Art," with *Open Wings*, by Alfonso Teja Zabre; subsequently, Virginia Fábregas and Mercedes Navarro will continue bringing to the stage Mexican productions. The UDAD for its part, effects the reading of dramas, among which can be mentioned *French Swallow*, by Francisco Monterde, and *The Intruders,* by Carlos Barrera, the author of *The First Woman*. Monterde adroitly exploits an almost virgin genre in Mexico: the literary theater. In the conjunct it is cold and precise — with absolutely classic coldness and precision — and is subtle and modern in every detail. Beyond his work in the theater, his *Bibliography of the Theater in Mexico* — a work of many years of patient, zealous and honorable research, and one of the greatest works in the history of the national theater — and his criticism, reserve for him a lofty perch. If he does not yet effect the crystallization of criticism, he is, on the other hand, the most astute and modern theatrical critic of the moment and one of the innovators in this art. Barrera, our only translator of Ibsen, is also the author of a play which has not been printed or performed to this date marks in this century a beginning for the theater of the masses and a more clearly defined social theater when compared to the previous attempts: it is *Slaves*, written in 1915 and copyrighted in Mexico City in 1917. Although a work of the moment at the time of its creation, it is transcendental in its conclusions and anticipates one of the ultimate truths of the revolution: the sacrifice of its initiators, even if their characters are independent of real revolutionary action and constitute elaborations in the manner of concentric spirits of the period of transformation. It seems to me, after reading it, to be the most important of those written until today in that genre, with the advantage of being the most theatrically constructed among them. Its author points out to me the coincidence which concerns a matter very similar to one — a clash between capital and labor — which John Galsworthy was to write about in his play *Strife* in 1918.

In August of 1923 the Teatro Sintético appears, organized by Rafael M. Saavedra, Carlos González and Francisco Domínguez. This spectacle, classifiable within the stylistic genre, employs Mexican motifs in whose presentation harmony between the movements and speeches of the actors and the music and sets is sought. Only *The Broken Pitcher, The Chinita* and *A Forced Marriage,* by Rafael M. Saavedra with sets by Carlos González and music by Francisco Domínguez, reach the public. This movement is of short duration, and must not be confused with the so-called "Theater of the Bat" which occurs in 1924. The humorous dance of "The Old Men"; *The Offering,* a moving synthesis of the ceremony for the dead which is held in Janitzio; *Trucks,* "a fleeting vision"; the dance of the Moors; "Juana," "a synthetic poem" by Manuel Horta; *Mexican Night,* and *The Cupboard,* a ballet number, all make up the program of the first experiment. Excessively derived from the *Bat,* by Nikita Balieff, this Theater of the Bat is not the true form of expression needed either, nor does the most nationalistic effort of the Teatro Sintético continue perfecting it even though it may be a "toystore for the soul," according to Luis Quintilla, who organized it with Carlos González and Francisco Domínguez.

XVIII.   Open Air Theater at San Juan Teotihuacán *(Above)*
Open Air Theater at Suchil (Durango) during a performance *(Below)*

Courtesy of Mr. Rafael M. Saavedra

XIX. Comic dance of
"The Old Men" *(Top)*
Dance of the Moors
(Bottom)

Courtesy of Mr.
Rafael M. Saavedra

XX. Sister Adoration of
the Divine Word, by Ju-
lio Jiménez Rueda, at the
Teatro Municipal *(Below)*

Courtesy of Mr. Ju-
lio Jiménez Rueda

XXI. *Orpheus,* by Jean Cocteau at the Teatro de Ulises *(Above)*

Courtesy of Xavier Villaurrutia

XXII. *Festival of Fire (Xiuhtzitzqui-lo),* a ballet by Antonio Gomezanda *(Below left)*

Courtesy of Mr. Antonio Go-mezanda

XXIII. Costume and mask of Quet-zalcoatl, by Carlos González from the ballet of the same name *(Below right)*

Courtesy of the Secretariat of Public Education

XXIV. Scenery by Carlos González for *Emiliano Zapata*
(Teatro de Ahora) *(Above)*

*Courtesy of Mauricio Magdaleno
and Juan Bustillo Oro*

XXV. Set by Carlos González for *Those Who Return*
(Teatro de Ahora) *(Below)*

*Courtesy of Juan Bustillo and Mau-
ricio Magdaleno*

Among other authors, Ermilo Abreu Gómez and Jacobo Dalevuelta (R. Ramírez de Aguilar) later furnished works for the Teatro Sintético.

After several isolated performances, some done by national actors and others by foreign ones, a Pro Arte Nacional season is begun which is carried on by the UDAD in conjunction with Alberto Tinoco, with an outstanding effort being made for the Pro Arte by the so-called Group of Seven (Francisco Monterde, José Joaquín Gamboa, Ricardo Parada León, Carlos Noriega Hope, Carlos and Lázaro Lozana García and Víctor Manuel Díez Barroso). According to reports no less than fifty Mexican works were brought to the stage during that season, with some consisting of synthetic theater. Fashion dictates. Other than the authors cited from that season, the following deserve mention; María Luisa Ocampo, José Luis Velasco, Ermilo Abreu Gómez, Julio Jiménez Rueda, Angel Marín and others. Among the works were *Control Yourself,* by Víctor Manuel Díez Barroso, which was awarded a prize in the theatrical contest sponsored in that year by the magazine *El Universal Ilustrado,* and the continuous duration of the movement lasts for seven months. Among the actors were Ricardo Mutio, Felipe Montoya, Paz Villegas, Matilde Cires Sánchez, Dolores Tinoco and others.

Organized by the writer María Luisa Ocampo, together with the Group of Seven, another run is carried out at the Teatro Fábregas in 1926 in which works by these authors and some foreigners are produced. The financial result for one reason or another is not satisfactory, which naturally interrupts it at the end of one hundred days.

An early movement of a literary nature is carried out in 1928 under the name Teatro de Ulises. It is a group of writers and poets who are, at the same time, actors, translators and stage directors: Salvador Novo, Xavier Villaurrutia, Gilberto Owen, Rafael Niteo, Ignacio Aguirre, Carlos Loquín and Delfín Ramírez Rovar, all of whom are assisted by Isabella Corona, Lupe Medina de Ortega, Clementina Otero and Emma Anchondo. Roberto Montenegro, Julio Castellanos and Manuel Rodríguez Lozano are the set designers, and the directors are Celestino Gorostiza, Julio Jiménez Rueda, Novo and Villaurrutia. It is not yet a matter of a nationalistic theater in the ritual sense of the word. The works

which are performed are not, of course, national ones: *The Res-
plendent Door,* by Lord Dunsany (translation by Enrique Jiménez
Domínguez); *Simili,* by Claude-Roger Marx (translation by Gilberto
Owen); *Welded,* by Eugene O'Neill — the first work by him
performed in Mexico — (with translation by Salvador Novo); *The
Pilgrim,* by Charles Vildrac (translation by Gilberto Owen); *Orpheus,* by the enfant terrible Jean Cocteau (translation by Corpus
Barga), and *Time is a Dream,* by H. R. Lenormand (translation by
Celestino Gorostiza and Antonieta Rivas). This theatrical experi-
ment consists of two runs: the first in a private theater, located
on Mesones Street, and the second in the Teatro Virginia Fábregas.

In the case of the Teatro de Ulises, as well as in all cases of
the theater in Mexico, a typically factorial spirit intervened which
limited the run and voided the effort expended. I understand that
the most literarily inclined segment of the public, trained for
criticism, did not wish to see the actors with the masks of the
various characters that they interpreted, but considered the intellectual or private personality of each one with scrupulous attention,
and that not only were the boundaries which separate the audience
from the characters violated, but those which separate the characters from those who impersonate them. The result was a radical
modification of the classical rules: life belonged to the actors and
not to the characters in the plays: the latter were forgotten because
of the attention paid to the former. I recall in passing that Eleonora
Duse refused on one occasion to hasten during an intermission to
the box of Marguerite of Savoy, Queen of Savoy. She expressed the opinion that in the theater the only visible part of her was
the actress.

There are several Mexican dramas which are staged, but they
are only a small proportion: among them there is *The Underdogs,*
an adaptation of the novel by Dr. Mariano Azuela, done by Antonieta Rivas and a Mr. Ituarte, and performed at the Teatro
Hidalgo (1929).

There is another season which is begun in 1929 with the name
Comedia Mexicana which is promoted by the writer Amalia G. C.
de Castillo Ledón and sponsored by the attorney Emilio Portes
Gil, President of the Republic, which lasts, divided between the
Teatro Regis and the Ideal, for about six months. As in the pre-
ceding ones, there are works by Parada León, María Luisa Ocam-

po, Díez Barroso, José Joaquín Gamboa, Noriega Tope, etc. The
first work of Parada León which was produced had as a title
Other People's Sorrows. The publicity aroused by the accusation
of plagiarism brought by the Nicaraguan novelist and dramatist
Hernán Robleto, currently the theatrical columnist of the morning
newspaper "El Universal Gráfico," against Parada León, was utilized
to its advantage. The work of Parada León is a poignant scenic
manifestation on the essential and previously mentioned basis of
the human element in this dramatist, and it offers, in fact, points
of consideration similar to those in the work by Hernán Robleto
(*The Lady Who Threw Off the Veil*). The similarity of situation
is evident. However the complication of the plot is based on the
cases of two equally respected authors whose backgrounds up to
that time are completely honorable. They give to the Mexican
their previous works which make of him one of the subjects of
concern to the theater. The Nicaraguan is supported by his integrity
and his continuity in literary and journalistic endeavors. Matters
concerning printed works in whose colophons truth finds itself seated
on its classical throne aside, a single error of salmonic affiliation
seems to be possible; all works emanate from an idea; the form
which they are given is charged with perpetuating them at a certain
level in the intellectual world; form is the defense of ideas, and
it should be observed that frequently they are best defended when
they are at their worst; authors frequently find themselves sacrificed
for their ideas. The idea of these works will perhaps sacrifice one
of the two writers; one of the two plays may disappear, leaving
room for the originality of the other. Time does justice in the
manner of the great feudal lords. Furthermore, I believe that both
works can survive and even be joined together, beyond the authors,
by the idea that generated them. If it is true that I definitively
refuse to listen to the voice of Anatole France concerning plagiarism, I do believe, on the other hand, that originality is restive
and mobile and as perfidious as... and that it cannot ever be
completely subjugated. I believe that there are examples of plagiarism, but I do not believe in plagiarism.

Amalia G. C. de Castillo León began also in 1929, by direction
of the Central Department of the Federal District, a series of
theatrical activities under the name of Popular Recreations, which
consisted of schools, parks, workers' centers and penal establish-

ments, and also including drama contests for the workers. In collaboration with this movement, Bernardo Ortiz de Montellano created and directed the puppet theater called "The Periquillo," which operated in parks and playgrounds for the entire year. The fabrication and animation of the puppets and the sets of the "Periquillo" were the responsibility of the Guerrero brothers and the painter Julio Castellanos. The work of Mrs. Castillo Ledón involved the installation of several temporary buildings, among them one named "Morelos" which was located at the entrance to the suburb of La Bolsa and was the first to be erected. The plans were drawn up by the architect Carlos Obregón Santacilia, and the decoration of the site was the responsibility of Diego Rivera. This temporary building is collapsible and has the only revolving stage in Mexico. Performances for workers, which included performances by workers, were held on Saturday nights, and Francisco Monterde's play *Workers* was the first one done. The actress Gloria Iturbe figured in the inauguration. It is also appropriate to mention the installation of an open air theater in Balbuena which was inaugurated with the performance of a pantomime entitled *Liberation,* which was a synthesis of Mexican history with sets by the painter Carlos González and a group of one thousand actors consisting of members of workers' organizations and inmates of correctional schools. This entire movement was carried out by the State, and it is the first and only one of its kind that has been done under those conditions.

To the cluster of works made up of those by the authors cited, it is necessary to add *The Strength of The Weak,* by Antonio Mediz Bolio, and the productions of the new authors who arise in this period: *When the Leaves Fall,* by Amalia G. C. de Castillo Ledón, and *Father Merchant* and *Over There Beyond the Mountains,* by Carlos Díaz Dufoo, Sr. *Among Brothers,* by Federico Gamboa, is produced out of season at about the same time by the dramatic company of the Argentine Actress Camila Quiroga.

There are two fleeting seasons in 1931: one at the Teatro Arbeu and the other at the Teatro Esperanza Iris. At the former, works by Miguel Bravo Reyes and others are produced, and at the latter, which is also the theater of the Comedia Mexicana, plays by María Luisa Ocampo and Carlos Díaz Dufoo, Sr. are staged.

In June of the same year the "Friends of the Mexican Theater" society is founded, which brings together all the literary writers

— the only ones lacking in the theater — and lovers of the dramatic art in general, whose plans, which include experimental undertakings and training for actors, are formulated from the most diverse sources. Perhaps the first great dramatic conservatory of Mexico will come into existence as a result of it.

The Secretariat of Public Education establishes in 1931 under its jurisdiction, although without great enthusiasm, the Teatro Orientación whose name is still not justifiable, in which only three works have been presented: two foreign ones and *Proteus,* by Francisco Monterde.

Finally, with the play *Emiliano Zapata* by Mauricio Magdaleno, the season of the so-called Theater of Today is begun at the Teatro Hidalgo on February 12, 1932. Magdaleno and Juan Bustillo Oro — who produced an adaptation of *Volpone* by Ben Jonson with the title Shark — are young new writers who, while searching like everyone else for the formula, have oriented themselves toward a political theater which may become in Mexico an equivalent of the theater of Erwin Piscator in Germany. There is as yet no technical revolution in this movement; but it is because there is not yet a total domination of the classical bases of the theater. Perhaps there will be later, why not? The season of the Theater of Today lasted for five weeks, and there was produced in it, beside the works already mentioned, *Pánuco 137* by Magdaleno and *Those Who Return,* the tragedy of the Mexican workers repatriated from the United States by Bustillo Oro.

All these latter efforts originated, in general, because of a nascent understanding of theatrical truth, for they are the work of the dramatists themselves. That is half of the secret. The writer should not live outside the theater for the same reason that the mechanic should not live far from machines. The experiments that have been pointed out do not form a crystallization; however, they can be considered as the first rational attempts, and are the best oriented to appear in the history of the theater of the Republic. This moment has another characteristic of equal importance: several types of authors are now relied upon; with dramatists who, although isolated from each other, become more refined in the wake of the general effort in a homogeneous way. For the first time in Mexico a classification may be made and the literary theater, the social theater, the regional theater, the *costumbrista* theater and perhaps the psychological theater, as well as the theater with goals of a purely theatrical nature, may be spoken about. It is evidently a question of embryos, but it is at least a matter of organized embryos.

Other authors such as Alfonso Reyes, Carlos Díaz Dufoo, Jr., Bernardo Ortiz de Montellano — who has specialized in the puppet theater —, Celestino Gorostiza, Xavier Icaza, José Gorostiza, Mariano Azuela, Antonio Helú, Joaquín Méndez Rivas, Aquiles Elorduy, Alfonso Gutiérrez Hermosillo (*Jacob's Ladder*), among the principal ones, figure on the second great theatrical era of Mexico together with those mentioned previously. Julia Nava de Ruisánchez, the first woman writer of the century to produce children's theater since 1913 (*Lotus Seed*, etc.), should also be mentioned.

The opera, a little neglected here as in the rest of the world, relies on works by Julián Carrillo: *Ossian* and *Matilde*, which are unpublished; by Rafael J. Tello: *Two Loves*, with libretto by Eduardo Trucco (1915); by José F. Vásquez: *Citlali* (1922, awarded a prize in competition), *The Mandarin* (1927), *The Rajah* (1929, performed in Guatemala) and *The Last Dream*, with librettos by Manuel M. Bermejo, and *The Miners*, unpublished, with libretto by Andrés Molina Enríquez; by Fausto Pinelo Río: *Payambé*, libretto by Luis Rosado Vega (1929). The plantation opera by Antonio Gómezanda entitled "The Virgin of San Juan," which is unpublished, constitutes a novelty in its genre and may be the beginning of a new, more sincere orientation in the national opera.

Another genre has emerged which is in perfect harmony with the Mexican spirit: the ballet. Starting with *Festival of Fire (Xiuhtziztquilo)*, an Aztec ballet with story by Francisco Monterde and music by Antonio Gómezanda — which is performed in Berlin on February 19, 1928 at the Nollendorfplatz Theater with costumes by José C. Tovar — there can be counted among the most outstanding: *Faunesque Scenes*, performed at the Teatro Regis in 1929 by the dance troupe of Miss Carroll, and *The Toloache*, a fantastic ballet from Oaxaca, both by Antonio Gómezanda; *Quetzalcoatl*, story by Rubén M. Campos, music by Alberto Flacheba and wardrobe, sets and masks by Carlos González; *Eight Hours*, story by Carlos González and music by José Pomar; *The Offering*, an Aztec ballet which has not been performed, by José F. Vásquez, based on a story by Manuel M. Bermejo, and *The*

New Fire and *H.P.*, by Carlos Chávez Ramírez, the last, a sim-
phony-ballet, was presented on March 31, 1932 by the Philadelphia
Grand Opera Company in the Metropolitan Opera House, in Philadelphia, with Leopold Stokowski conducting. The sets and costumes
were the work of Diego Rivera, and the choreography was directed
by Catherine Littlefield.

The regional theater of Yucatán, a hybrid in two languages
— Maya and Spanish — which has been mentioned previously, takes
on important proportions in its turn. Among the most outstanding
authors are Esteban Rejón Tejeda, José Talavera, José Brito, Juan
Pérez, Alfredo Tamayo, Alejandro Cervera, Alvaro Zavala. Their
works are only dramatic scenes based on legends and regional traditions, and in them ethnic, ethical and political problems together
with racial conflicts, and never any theme of love, are treated.
Since the authors compose no dialogues, it is the *mestizo* actors
who improvise them on the stage, reviving one of the probable
means of operation of the ancient theater of Yucatan and Mexico
and continuing, in spite of poor Goldoni, the joy of the *commedia
dell'arte.*

Furthermore, Yucatan has produced dramatists prolifically:
beside Peón y Contreras, it has José Antonio Cisneros and José
Cisneros Cámara in the nineteenth century and Mediz Bolio, Arturo Peón Cisneros, Gonzalo Pat y Valle, Delio Moreno Cantón,
Ermilo Abreu Gómez — to whom I am grateful for all the information concerning Yucatan which is contained in this chapter — and
many more in the twentieth century.

The modern theatrical influence which seems to have been reflected to a greater degree on the technique of the theater in
Yucatan is that of Antonio García Gutiérrez, who — a fact which
I also owe to Abreu Gómez — lived in Yucatan in 1847, having
written during his stay in the region a drama entitled *The Mayors
of Valladolid,* based on a local legend from the eighteenth century.

Although the several movements mentioned make of the last
ten years the first of the century with regard to theatrical matters,
the lack of unity among them, in spite of the previously cited ho-
mogeneity of effort, is still evident. If they can be considered
separately as efforts at national expression, they do not comprise
any efforts of national expression. Among one another there are
differences of points of departure, and there does not appear in

them a single characteristic which binds them together. Their aims, when not dissimilar, are opposed to each other and mutually exclude each other. However, there has been arising among the writers — particularly the poets — a new interest in the theater which is increased by the very preponderance of the cinematographer, who seems less today than ever to be the definitive expression of contemporary races. The industry is becoming wealthy, but it only expresses a materialistic thrust. The United States is now trying to become the great artistic and literary marketplace as well — a bad habit caused by its puerile love of championships — because it knows that unless it does it cannot be fulfilled or express itself in an absolute fashion by means of the cinematographer. Consequently the theater is beginning to be regarded anew here and there by eyes that understand better because they have seen more.

But the affluence of the dramatists which is more evident in recent years notwithstanding, and the conditions of orientation which still exist aside, there is another aspect of the theater which has not even evolved in the same proportion as the dramatist.

The Actors

A desert of stage directors and trained actors confronts the scrutiny of the new playwrights who know that this is the moment to forge ahead and to prepare the beginnings of the Mexican theater.

If theatrical tourism was brilliant in the nineteenth century, in the twentieth it has been no less so. [1] As is the case in the former, neither has that in the latter benefited our actors considerably.

The lack of institutions with quasi-monastic regulations is deplorable — such as the theatrical school founded in Russia in 1779 by Catherine II, or like the modern Russian ballet studios, or like Piscator's studio in Germany — in which theatrical actors might be trained to carry to the faraway shore of the public the lofty ideals and beautiful forms which the creators are preparing on the opposite shore.

---

[1] See the "Chronological Resumé of the Theater in Mexico" at the back of this volume, pp. 153-172, for the first third of the twentieth century.

In order to define the actor it is necessary to introduce Richard Burbage here, the animator of the principal inhabitants of the planet Shakespeare. George Bernard Shaw says: "...and the man about whom we are told that when he wanted to say that Richard had died and he shouted: 'A Horse! A horse!' he called for Burbage, was the father of nine generations of Shakespearian spectators, all of whom spoke about the Richard of Garrick, the Othello of Kean, the Shylock of Irving and the Hamlet of Forbes Robertson without knowing nor worrying about whether these works had anything to do with the *Richard,* the *Othello,* etc., of Shakespeare."

Then Oscar Wilde says: "The actor is the critic of the drama."

The first definition represents glory, and the second the spirit of the dramatic career.

The European conservatories have tried, I suppose, to teach to the many what the few possessed and had to transmit to them to insure the continuation of the dramatic art, which follows after music in popularity and in power. Hence there would come from them finished products, temperaments refined to the point of theatrical perfection who would unleash their true struggle upon the commercial theaters. In them flourished or took flight the greatest artistic vocations to the extent that it could be said that in the theater — as in any art — the few who loved the theater survived and triumphed while those who only loved the illusion of the theater disappeared forever. In those conservatories there has been studied in the light of all methods a national theater in whose structure, floor by floor, there appear all the embellishments and all the refinements of language and, apart from the acting, gestures and diction, one learned in them to recognize the very soul of language and its uninterrupted advance toward purity, balance, grace, precision and musical crystallization.

The result was the disappearance of those delightful adventurers who became actors in *The Captain's Failure,* the exile of Captain Spavento, and the *auto de fe* of the *commedia dell'arte.* It was not sufficient just to have an inclination or to fall in love with an actress in order to gain admission into the theater, This was the beginning of modern life: it was necessary to have an education. Genial temperaments are, furthermore, the only ones which are able to subject themselves to a discipline without being destroyed. The sensitive actor has lived his role who has, because he perceives it thus, shouted when it is necessary to feign authority, wept when it is necessary to feign sorrow — as if sorrow and tears were one and the same thing — and he says "Brrr!" when he has to pretend that he is cold. The theater educated itself just as children and democracy educated themselves in order to assure themselves of a long and respectable life. In this way the classical requirements, which rightly insisted that the dramatist be at the same time a critic, actor, stage director or empresario, and the modern requirement which this culture demands, which is the *mal-du-siecle,* are joined together.

And Mexico?

On the one hand there are the foreign actors — generally Spaniards — who brought with them in their immigration European schools and fashion, and on the other our temperamental actors, twisted and deformed on the anvil of habit, who were imitating the Spanish and are imitating them even today in order to be admitted into the only great theater of the Spanish-speaking world — a statement which is made for purposes of classification — and in order to be esteemed by the public, which is beginning not to be able to tolerate them now.

Generally those among our actors and actresses to whom the good fortune was given to learn their profession at the side of the most reknowned figures of the Spanish theater did not understand what their role should be. Instead of assimilating, they imitated. Generally none of them hesitated in bringing to his country that which, even though valid in Spain, turned out to be false here. Generally none seems to have kept anything of his own personality for the return trip, and they give the impression of having paid for the learning of an exotic intonation and an artificial pronunciation with it. Reputed to be the best, however, they saw themselves regaled with the loftiest positions of the theatrical art. And the fans and devotees who had not gone to Europe then imitated the former in order, in their turn, to become masters of an art in which spirit and form were in such an overwhelming discord that it was no longer a matter of an art, but of a total imbalance.

In the Conservatory, as has been seen, the Spanish theater imposed itself — the Colonial domination thus prolonging itself once more — as well as the school of uniform sonority in whose domain, also Spanish, one can be sublime and often ridiculous, even Mexican. The remainder of those studies is somewhat unpleasant: contaminated professors, even if they are not foreign in the main, hostility toward perfect phonetics with its *c,* its *z* and its *ll,* and at times — worse yet — toward the regional pronunciations of Spain in that theatrical branch of modern life which is, fortunately, almost already extinct. It has been shown — relatively speaking — that a good education makes good temperaments sublime, and that a bad one makes them mediocre and vapid. Almost all the good minds came out of that conservatory of Spanish conventions annihilated and were rejected by the professional theater. The same works were produced on the public stages and studied at the Conservatory. In the former Spanish actors performed them; in the latter minds were tainted, its products had an aroma of artificiality and dullness, a false and perverse character. Naturally one must enunciate clearly when acting in a Spanish play; but there Castilian pronunciation was extended to translations of plays from all languages, and to Mexican dramas as if we were in old Spain. And we were not even in the new one.

The contrast between a brief conversation in the wings — which was sincere, spontaneous and very Mexican — and the artificial and "learned" speech of the actors on stage was deplorable, and it was reflected in one attitude or another with regrettable results. I also had to use the Castilian *c, z,* and *ll* — directed to do so, naturally, by a Mexican professor — in the works of Echegaray and the Quintero brothers as well as in the translations of d'Annunzio, in *Manelik,* by Antonio Mediz Bolio, and in the Mexican *sainetes* in the playhouse of Lechuga. I am convinced that such a keen obsession is only equalled by the effort expended on the wearing of one's first black tie, which consequently prevents one from feeling free to dance, flirt or eat at a soiree. One raises his hands to touch it so frequently that it ends by being soiled, or by having its beautiful harmony totally damaged. A smile from one's date, from an acquaintance passing by, or worse yet from an obsequious host, upsets the unfortunate debutant and sends him desperately scurrying in search of a mirror in front of which, in the end, he is fatally surprised. All of this is further aggravated generally by the fact that most of us do not know how to tie our first black tie and therefore require maternal assistance or the

scoffing and tender aid of our sisters. In this same manner that
phonetic pulchritude which often pushed its victim into the abyss
of a broad *ceceo* was equally ridiculous. It was, in addition, a great
waste of time, a continual stagnation and daily immolation of
acting, of the plot — at times of the vocation — in tribute to the
imported diction.

There was a time, however, in which the activity of the Conservatory experienced unusual promise. In the course of the second
decade of the twentieth century the students staged Mexican and
foreign works with relative frequency. Of all the names which
considered themselves fixed forever in the treacherous columns of
the newspapers almost none remains. Among the few surviving,
many have fallen into the mortal trap of the burlesque theater,
dragged down by a crippled sense of vocation; some have come
to know the antiquated and thorny halo of the tent shows. Some
few, diverted but disciplined in their deviation, support themselves
decorously in second, third or fourth rate locations.

The students, realizing the absolute uselessness of taking courses
in theatrical arts — courses better suited for hobbies than for
careers — intelligently went home for the most part; others became
musicians, singers or pharmacists, and others, thinking that they
would find artistic autonomy there, scurried to the shelter of
teaching positions in declamation. Reciting is a difficult thing, it is
the creation of poetry from diction; but to recite badly is something
instinctive, it is like singing off-key or adding sums incorrectly. It
is markedly so following the harmonious visit to this country of
Bertha Singermann — who does not recite — which has caused
abject confusion. She has been copied and mimicked without decorum and without success. All the known schools of declamation
in Mexico were thrown off balance by her exceptional ability, and
it as at that time that the Conservatory rid itself of the arts of
the theater and declamation. The rest was only a simple objective
and bureaucratic formula: suppressing classifications, signing com-
muniques, terminating professors, et cetera. Here lies the School of
Dramatic Art and Declamation...

On the other hand, we are in debt to the revue for innumerable
improvisations by tiny sopranos and even smaller choristers. The

calves of some legs, deftly turned by the busy secular chisel, have found easier ways to orient their talent for movement than has a mentality to develop itself. Legs have in their domain, like music and painting, an international language. Furthermore, since a genuine musical education takes too much time, the revue associated itself with the democratic order of things; it made sacrifices and concessions to the liking of the public, and its attraction descended from the throat to the legs. I suppose that it can go no lower, and that it will have to rise again or disappear.

It is also necessary to admit that Mexican actors have followed the modern rhythm by unionizing themselves. Our groups of that type date from 1916, which proves that they were not completely backward. Their excision of the "C.R.O.M." later (1930), again shows them to be well versed in social matters.

If it is true that we have witnessed in Mexico several lofty theatrical masterpieces, it is no less true that nations cannot live on masterpieces alone. A communality is necessary which, by mandate of the people from remotest times, is polished and smooth to the extreme of being, if such a thing can be said, an exceptional commonplace. Professional weakness, pallor and failure in the professional theater imply that the future depends on a theater of experimentation which will utilize in an adequate manner the undiverted talents and training which has yet to be accomplished. The labor will be long; but Mexico is young. Apart from Virginia Fábregas we have only had at the highest levels of our theater María Luisa Villegas and Dora Vila, both of whom are now deceased, the latter having passed away in 1925 while she was working in Spain; and María Teresa Montoya. After Francisco Cardona, who died in 1913, we had Fernando Soler — who has already left the theater for the cinema — and we have Alfredo Gómez de la Vega, whose season at the Teatro Arbeu in 1930 still seems to have been unforgettable if not perfect. Gómez de la Vega also believes in the need for a renovation on the basis of new elements. The majority of the artists who worked beside him at that time came from amateur dramatic groups: Gloria Iturbe — alone in this group which contained the sum total of the actress —, Isabella Corona, Alberto Galán. Others had worked previously before paying audiences abroad such as Miguel Ángel Ferriz, who has not completely received his due. Others came directly from within themselves such as Andrea Palma. These

names are, up to now, the only ones heading toward the future of
the theater in Mexico. They are the exception in other genres: Esperanza Iris, the successor to Adelina Velu and Amparo Romo in
the Viennese operettas; Beristáin, Soto and Lupe Rivas Cacho,
previously mentioned, in the revue, a genre which except for Joaquín
Pardavé seems to be headed for oblivion in the near future.

With greater frequency, of course, we have seen luminous figures
in the opera. Although we may only include a few after Ángela
Peralta and Madame Ochoa de Miranda, the remainder are still
worthwhile. María de Jesús Magaña, Beatriz Franco, María de la
Fraga, Ángela Aranda, the wife of the celebrated Didour; Soledad
Goyzueta, José Vigil y Robles, José Torres Ovando, Felipe Llera,
Lelo de Larrea, Gustavo Bernal, Saldaña, José Servín and others
delighted lovers of the opera since the turn of the century. Then
Fanny Anitúa, María Luisa Escobar de Rocabruna, Consuelo Esco-
bar de Castro, Josefina Llaca, Carmen García Cornejo, Ada Navarrete, María Romero, Manuel Romero Malpica, Carlos Mejía,
Rodolfo Hoyos, María Teresa Santillán, Eduardo Lejarazu, David
Silva, Ángel Esquivel, Alfonso Ortiz Tirado and many more who
have honorably preserved the tradition of the great lyrical genre
appeared.

In all the arts there exists the danger of disappearing if no lasting
works are produced, but in none so imminently as in the theater.
Eleonora Duse, that phenomenon of the modern theater, was aware
of this. A pen more expert than mine in the anecdotal history of
the theater in Mexico will have to record many of the names which
I do not mention, and which certainly deserve to survive from that
point of view.

It is difficult to define which of the artist's activities is the most
important: whether to create art or never to stop definitively. It
is difficult particularly when dealing with the actor. There is no
lack of people who maintain that the world's greatest painters have
achieved their greatest works more because of necessity than out of
inspiration. It may seem similarly to be the case in matters concerning the actor who is obliged to a greater degree to please the
public in order to live. But in art, as in love, excessive pleasure
wanes and, nevertheless, in no other artist is the need for continued
evolution so imperative.

The poet who has shut himself away in a minor school later sees his efforts justified, to a certain degree, by the permanence of his work as a link in an evolutionary chain, as a representative of an intermediary period between the primitive mind and the decadent mind, and he is an indispensable historical element. This poet is the one who, during his time, pleases the public. The actor who limits himself in a similar way is immediately forgotten after his death or retirement, if he is not forced to retire or to die. He leaves behind no justification whatsoever for his need to limit himself: he does not even receive the attention given to the artists in another genre who represent a necessary transition. When a poet can no longer receive into himself the force of a new trend, when he is exhausted, he has then completed his work, no matter what the amount of artistic volume it may have attained. When an actor can no longer take upon himself a character whose traits are those of a new human evolution he is exhausted, and nothing that he has done previously can keep him from dying. He will be remembered pleasantly or unpleasantly by his aged contemporaries, but no one else will ever hear of him again. In short, there is no artist who is required to please the public more than the actor; none with greater need than he not to displease it. There is no passion between the artist and the audience as complicated as that which concerns the actor. When a passion ceases it dies. And the duty of the actor is to nourish it until he is consumed by it, because only in this way can he attain survival. I regret it, but that is the way that it is.

On the other hand, I must admit that the study of music and singing has been sown at the National Conservatory with a bountiful harvest. The students of singing end by becoming teachers or by joining the choral backdrop of the opera, and the instrumentalists generally join the Symphonic Orchestra. Mexico has three very pronounced artistic conditions: it is a melomaniacal country and a great admirer of colour and design. This accounts for the intense development of musical, pictorial, architectural and plastic endeavors; the progress of the open air painting schools and those of sculpture, of the efforts of all the schools to encourage children, and of concerts in general. But this does not mean that Mexico cannot enjoy the theater as well. The very fact that it does not have it indicates that it needs it. The success of the foreign troupes — even now — and the support of various Mexican ones, some mediocre and others damaged by a discouraging heterogeneity, as well as the applause awarded the theatrical highlights, emanate — like the complaints and the flight to the movie houses — from a popular appetite which has remained unsatisfied up until the present time.

The Motion Picture

It is the motion picture which has had the greatest impact on the theater in Mexico. I have purposely excluded politics. I do not know whether this fact is the result of the failure of the motion picture or not, which necessitates no further comments.

I will not presume, furthermore, to do more than present a brief resume.

The motion picture began to receive the attention of audiences in Mexico in 1906. Its popularity begins in 1912 with European films. In that year the Teatro Principal closes — on the occasion of the dismissal of the Arcaraz Company — after an uninterrupted run of more than twenty years in the *género chico* which resulted in its consecration as the Cathedral of Vaudeville. In his history, José Juan Tablada celebrates the death of vaudeville and the coronation of the cinematographer, whom he calls — and we shall resist commenting — the Zola of the imaginary. The truth is that the cinema has always been an enigma.

The first Mexican motion picture does not appear until 1917. It is an attempt at technical innovation and is almost the only film done without theatrical elements: it is *Light,* an interpretation by Emma Padilla. Afterward it is a theatrical artist who carries out the first organized attempt. Mimí Derba founds Aztec Films, also in 1917. With her Joaquín Coss, a long-time actor, assumes the task of cinematographic director; María Caballé, Emilia del Castillo, Matilde Cires Sánchez, Julio Taboada, Ernesto Finance and others, *zarzuela* and dramatic actresses, all become movie actors. At this time the following films are made: *In Self Defense, Soul of Sacrifice* and *The Daydreamer.* The last is written and directed by the theatrical actor Eduardo Arozamena, and Natalia Ortiz, the dramatic actress, also appears in it. The opera company which consisted at the beginning of Rosa Raisa, Ana Fitziu, Ricardo Stracciari, Zenatello, Andrea de Segurola and others, was in

Mexico City at about the same time and, at the insistence of Mimí Derba, took part in the film *The Daydreamer*. In short, the theatrical element predominates.

Other films are made: *Tepeyac*, based on the legend of the Virgin of Guadalupe, with Pilar Cota and José Manuel Ramos; *The Wound* and *Saint*, adapted from the novels of Federico Gamboa, in which María Mercedes Ferriz and Elena Sánchez Valenzuela, students at the School for Theatrical Art, respectively perform: *María*, a motion picture version of the novel by Jorge Isaacs, if performed by Gilda Chávarri; *El Zarco*, based on the novel by Altamirano, has in its cast Lygia de Golconda and Graciela de Zárate. The journalist Alfonso Bussón also performs in *Saint*.

The professional theater turns to the cinema later. Leopoldo Beristáin films *Round Trip* aided by nearly all of his collaborators from the folkloric theater: Lucina Joya, Joaquín Pardavé, the Iglesias brothers and Alicia Pérez...

Among other films, there emerge *Tabaré*, a motion picture version of the poem by Zorrilla de San Martín, and *Don Juan Manuel*, a colonial legend of Mexico, both done by Alfonso Castilla; *Civil Death*, done by Alejandro de Mezzi together with the opera singer María Luisa Escobar and the soprano Lupe Rivas Cacho. Following these productions, the series which constitutes the most solid advance in the cinema of Mexico appears. The enterprise owned by Germán Camus, which imports motion pictures, erects the first complete studio and produces six films, two of which are adaptations of theatrical works: *After Death*, by José Manuel Othón, and *At the Hacienda*, by Federico Carlos Keggel. The theatrical actors, except for Antonio Galé, are no longer involved in this activity. A group of purely cinematographic figures are in Camus' cast: Elmira Ortiz, Lygia de Golconda, Emma Padilla, Carmen Bonifant, Aída Verda, Guillermo Hernández, Armando Bolio Avila, Enrique Cantalauba, Eduardo Martorell and others. The sets, wardrobe and part of the artistic direction are handled by the painter Carlos González.

However, in *Tragic Confession*, an adaptation of a poem by José Velarde which is filmed by amateurs, María Mercedes Ferriz, who later will limit herself exclusively to being a dramatic actress, plays the principal role. Joaquín Coss, Miguel Ángel Ferriz, Ernesto Finance and Dora Vila all perform later in *The Gray Automobile*, a serial inspired by the trial of the gang of the same name, and Matilde Cires Sánchez, Roberto Soto and others appear in *The Automobile Gang,* a serial based on the former film. In the film version done by Alfredo B. Cuéllar of a novel by Cosmo Hamilton (*The Scandal*), figures from the theater are also present: the actress Emilia del Castillo and Enrique Tovar Avalos, professor of declamation at the School of Theatrical Art.

Another's Crime, produced by Stahl Brothers and performed by Amparo Rubio, Carlos Stahl and others; *Son of the Madwoman,* played by Adela Sequeyro — who also acts in *Social Scandal* together with the German actress Marr Teledo and the caricaturist Ernesto García Cabral —; *Rosario's Wedding* — in which Lupe del Hoyo, the Marquis of Guadalupe and the Cuban José Martínez Casado appear —, among other motion pictures, all were equally a part of the passing array.

The Corporal, performed by Miguel Contreras Torres and Delia Altamirano and *The Great News,* a picture filmed by journalists with the writer Cube Bonifant in the role of the protagonist with a story by Carlos Noriega Hope, deserve to be mentioned among the most recent productions of this type together with *Christ of Gold,* a work with a colonial theme performed by Otilia Zambrano and Luis Márquez in which the dramatic actress Fanny Schiller also takes part, which is under the direction of Basilio Zubiaur and Manuel R. Ojeda.

Joaquín Coss, Eduardo Arozamena, José Manuel Ramos — a poet and translator of dramatic works —, Ernesto Vollrath, Alfonso Castilla, Gustavo Sáenz de Sicilia, Cuéllar, Ojeda and Noriega Hope have all been motion picture directors. Jorge Stahl, Ezequiel Carrasco and others figure principally among the cameramen along with Roberto A. Turnbull and Enrique Vallejo, even though the last two have worked mainly in the United States.

Because of her specialization in the cinema, Elvira Ortiz, who was mentioned previously, deserves mention for her work in the studios of Camus where she performed, among other films, in *Amnesia,* which was based on the novel by Amado Nervo. It is a fine production, and is surely one of great promise in Mexican cinematography. Her premature death prevented her reaching Hollywood, which was not as open to the exotic productions of Mexico in those years. Nevertheless, Beatriz Domínguez, who also died in

her youth, was able to work there previously. Ramón Navarro, Dolores del Río, Manuel R. Ojeda, Miguel Contreras Torres, Fernando
R. Elizondo, also all belong to the motion picture colony.

Elsewhere, Lupe Vélez and Delia Magaña, like Arozamena,
Celia Montalván and others, have been taken away by Hollywood
in recent years. Fernando Soler, a theatrical actor and the only
Mexican to work in the studios in Joinville, France, and Virginia
Fábregas, who performed in the Spanish version of a film done in
English by the actress Marie Dressler (*The Bitter Fruit*), also belong
to this group.

Finally, in the motion picture *Saint,* a new cinematographic version of the novel by Federico Gamboa which is the first talking
picture made in Mexico, with dialogue by Carlos Noriega Hope
and directed by Antonio Moreno with a performance by Lupita
Tovar —who has also acted in Hollywood —, such theatrical actors
as Carlos Orellana, whose talent may carry him far beyond the
pathways of the Spanish astrakhan, appear. Mimí Derba, José Martínez Casado and others also perform in this film. The company
which produced *Saint* has just finished *Eagles in the Sun* and is
preparing its first classical Mexican film, based on the novel *Cle-
mencia* by Ignacio Altamirano, from an adaptation by Carlos Noriega Hope. This production will attempt to set a new trend inasmuch as it envisions the fusion of the most talented and diverse
segments from the artistic, literary and technical spheres collab-
orating in a series of works. The music will be under the direction
of Maestro Julián Carrillo.

Other small companies are slowly being formed, among them
Eco Film which will soon begin the filming of the Mexican legend
adapted by the dramatist Guz Aguila. In the month of June, 1932,
Miguel Contreras Torres, author of the recent motion picture *The
Dreamers of Glory,* began a new work entitled *The Mexican Revolution,* which aspires to contain the story of the revolutionary life
of Mexico. In her turn, the dramatic actress Gloria Iturbe is currently making films.

To the general movement towards film making can be added
organization of the Cinema Club of Mexico, which is engaged in
interesting activities under the direction of Emilio Amero, Bernardo
Ortiz de Montellano, Manuel Álvarez Bravo, Dolores Álvarez
Bravo, María Izquierdo, Roberto Montenegro and Federico Cannessi

together with Agustín Aragón Leiva as General Secretary. This group, which has ideas concerning the introduction of the educational film into Mexico, the production of Mexican artistic films and an attack on the "detestable spirit of Hollywood and its false and commercial motion picture industry," in spite of its intention to educate the masses, has the clear earmarks of a minority and as such will fulfill a need which was being progressively neglected in Mexico. It was founded on June 16, 1932 with a performance at the Bolívar Amphitheater of the outstanding film *The Process of Birth,* which was directed and photographed by Eduard Tissé and produced by Praessens Films, A. G., of Zurich, Switzerland.

It is curious to observe that if in the film industry in the United States such outstanding theatrical artists as Florence Reed and John Barrymore performed for many years, at the present the invasion of the dominions of the theater by the cinema is producing on a larger scale the movement already begun in Mexico. Although Ann Harding is constantly being mentioned, it is sufficient to cite, in order to prove the validity of such an assertion, the numerous singers, dancers and character actors who work in the contemporary motion picture industry in the United States, a career which is quite harmful to the operetta, the *zarzuela,* the dramatic theater and the opera itself.

In spite of the lack of development achieved up to this time by the film industry in Mexico, the future of the cinema seems less uncertain, in fact, than that of the theater which depends primarily on money, something which is currently difficult to obtain.

The Theater

The decline of the theater throughout the world is currently a widespread topic of conversation. Mexico is not an exception in this regard, of course, and the emptiness of the stages lends support to some who hold to this theory of the decline. Against them those who hold an opposing opinion dispute this statement, which they judge to be of a falacious nature: it is impossible for something to decline which has never fully existed.

Both sides verge on error. For once the arrangement of the factors alters the result. What in reality has happened, from the times of ancient Greece to the present, was not that the theater declined,

but that Greece entered into a period of decadence. But the theater
was able to go to Rome, and it went. The Middle Ages having
ended, the theater ceases to be religious, but it does not decline.
In its religious form it was the expression of the Middle Ages;
later it expresses the Renaissance in a fashion which is renascent.
The theater is the active expression of the diverse epochs of the
world, and in this way it runs the entire gamut.

The reason that the theater is not declining in Mexico lies in
the fact that Mexico is not a decadent country. The reason that the
theater may not be leading a perfect life, granted that Mexico is not
a decadent country, lies in the fact that it has still not reached full
development. In order for Mexico to follow the theater in its state
of definitive development, the theater needs primarily to follow
Mexico in its evolution. One type of decadence has already reigned
in Mexico: that of neolithic life. It was a gigantic decline. But now
a plenitude is lacking: that of a people which has been developing
with difficulty in the midst of Indian melancholy and the reverberations and foreign yokes of four centuries. A people which will later
decline.

It is stated that the theater is declining in the industrialized
countries. It is true that the decadence of a continent or of a country
which has ruled the life of the world for an era has repercussions
throughout the entire world. But this does not necessarily imply
universal decadence. The death of a grandfather may impress, sad-
den and disorient a grandson; but it does not age him or force him
to die at the same time. It reveals to him, as did his full life
previously, a future and final path. I do not believe, furthermore,
that this moment in the world is one of decadence. Until now
decadence has been wise and at times supreme in its expression.
We are disoriented, not exhausted. The concern of the entire world
is a prelude to the decadence of the machine; but not of anything
else. Nevertheless, even if there were a decline, the sunset in the
West does not have to be our sunset. When the sun can no longer
rise in Europe it will have to come up in America, because the sun
must rise. I am speaking of the Latin countries. The United States
offers itself to the observer as a transition without precedent in
the history of civilization, or at least until today.

Moreover, if it is true that art is not completely independent
of the medium, if it is the result of the productive refinement of a

nation and of the former or the tomb of the latter. It utilizes nations and peoples in order to limit itself — if it did not do this it could never express itself —, and once the former have disappeared it returns to its primitive condition as a limitless phenomenon until it can surround itself with new restrictions. The limitation are impulse, color and nationality, just as human, animal or vegetable bodies are the limitation and arrangement of life, just as society is the limitation of mankind or as nations are the limitations of societies. While in the old nations shaken by politics people speak about the decadence and vanity of art — which seems opposed to them because their events do not deserve to end like King Henry VIII in a volume by Shakespeare —, in the United States, for example, the return to art is beginning because art has something to say at this time in the United States. A theatrical mountain peak is emerging, therefore, beyond the plain of farces and the foothills of the *sainete*.

Spain, in its turn, although making an appeal on the basis of its classical theater, is beginning to undertake a theatrical campaign with mobile and stationary playhouses in which the juvenile disinterest of students and new actors is going to revive for the people the marvelous old spectacle in the style of Lope de Rueda by attempting to give to the ancient farce a simple modern appearance.

All of modern Russia, including Georgia and Armenia, is rising up in the face of the masses of today in the ancestral accoutrements of the stage in order to distribute not only a social doctrine, but that which art alone can give completely: concern on the one hand, serenity on the other; anguish with one mask and understanding with another.

In Germany the political theater is boiling; in France the experiments of the select minorities are taking place. In the whole world, in short, the theater is monopolizing public attention as never before in the old Modern Age.

The disorientation of a country in any artistic regard is only the unlimited aspect of some art form. It means that there is not yet in that country a group of men who are the product of a refined ethnical process, who are capable of mastering it with a firm hand; that the race of people in that country is not yet a resilient and adequate channel for the flow of that art form. It is true that in contrast to the sickly existence of the theater in Mexico there is the magnificent health of painting, for example. It is true as well that some forms of art are more suited to some peoples than others. But surely the theater is the ultimate art form. Its age is the same as that of the first civilization on earth. It has persisted in spite of the dissappearance of continents and the ruination of nations; in spite of the fact that it is neither sculpted nor painted; in spite of not always having been written down or printed. The actors spoke their lines and died; but they achieved a transcendental existence for centuries during which the album of the cinematographer did not yet exist.

During its entire frequently inconsistent and at times purely legendary history, the theater appears to have been characterized by something inevitable which, even if it is also manifested in all other art forms, is nowhere as forceful as in the theater. One might almost say that art is inevitable, but that the theater is fatal. No convincing reason has occurred to me which would exclude Mexico from the tradition of the theater.

Will the one which emerges in Mexico be a conventional theater, an open air theater, an aerial theater with front row clouds as the result of the profoundly new age upon which mankind is entering? It will probably have a classical foundation which will seem modern... It is all the same. The aesthetic needs of the people will surely be fulfilled when they cease to be the need for aesthetic exigencies and reach a level which will permit them to orient, direct and limit the expression of art. The artist is only a perceptive servant of those needs. At times he foresees them. Perhaps once every century or every epoch he creates them.

At any rate, theatrical expression will come when it has an absolute reason to exist, when it has something to say.

No art form dies because an artistic school subsides. Therefore neither the Greek schools, nor the Religious School, nor the Renaissance School did away with the theater. Movement and immobility have been able to manifest it. No school is the salvation or perdition of art. It is art which at times saves the schools.

In conclusion, the problem of the theater is no more urgent in Mexico than the ethnic problem. Neither of the two may be resolved in any experiment whose only function is to indicate causes and — on occasions — to forecast effects. They do not depend on any men, but on the man who stands out with greatest relief in some individuals when, like a limited living force in one race, he reaches an essential level. Beyond the fact that it is impossible to stop it, this does not mean that the efforts made by the theater in Mexico can be suspended or misdirected so that one may calmly wait for the race to be purified and to need and master some form of expression or other. On the contrary, they must be multiplied tenfold. We must hasten to produce inferior, colorless and ugly works if necessary so as to proceed more rapidly from them to stronger, colorful and beautiful ones. Follies which are not committed in youth are more doleful in middle age.

It is necessary, particularly, to declare a moratorium on definitions, to restrict criticism to the ambit of self-criticism, and to write less about the theater and more for the theater. Equilibrium requires a great deal of time and presents at times the danger of making shortcomings apparent which would be more beneficial if they went unnoticed.

Finally, the theatrical moment of Mexico will not be long in coming. It doubtlessly belongs to the next generation. It is impossible to put greater effort or greater sacrifice into the heritage which is being prepared for it, and its abundant and opulent result is destined to be the result of this effort and this sacrifice.

March, 1932

CHRONOLOGICAL RÉSUMÉ OF THE THEATER
IN MEXICO DURING THE FIRST THIRD
OF THE TWENTIETH CENTURY

1899

Esperanza Dimarías, Rosa Fuertes, Rosario Soler, whose stage name was "La Pata," and others figure in the *zarzuela* and the operetta.

Orrin Amphitheater. Opera company featuring Rosalía Chalía and Sigaldi. Success of *Fedora*, by Giordano.

Concerts by Luisa Ritter, pianist.

Concerts by the dramatic alto soprano Matilde Brugière.

The opera company of Napoleón Sieni performs with Adela Gini Pizzorni, Lea Sangiorgio, Adelina Padovani, etc.

Concerts directed by Maestro Carlos J. Meneses.

December. The Spanish dramatic troupe headed by María Guerrero and Fernando Díaz de Mendoza, which stages *Cyrano de Bergerac* in Mexico City, and produces *The Truth Suspected* by Juan Ruiz de Alarcón, among other works.

1900

January 7. The actress María de Jesús Servín dies.

Opening of the Teatro del Renacimiento. (Now the Virginia Fábregas.)

January 24. Presentation at the Teatro Nacional of the magician César Watry.

January 30. Concerts by Sofía Scalchi, the Pasqualis and Franceschetti.

March 10 and 11. Concerts by the pianist Ignatz Paderewski.

April. Performance by the hypnotist Onofroff, at the Nacional.

The Tomba Company performs *zarzuelas* with Elvira Lafón and others.

The opera *Atzimba,* by Ricardo Castro, is sung by Soledad Goyzueta, Esperanza Dimarías, Miss Vivanco, etc.

1901

Teatro Renacimiento. French opera company featuring Montbazon, Nina Pak, Miss Talexis and Jérome.

Demolition of the Gran Teatro Nacional.

Concerts by the pianist Teresa Carreño.

At the Teatro Renacimiento, Rosa Castillo, María Anaya, Josefina Roca de Chico, Leonor Delgado, Leonor Castillo, etc.

The dramatic company of Teresa Mariani arrives.

Italian opera company with Madame Turconi Bruni, Vinci, Rambaldi, Adriana Palermi, Lery, etc.

Concerts by the violinist María Schumann.

The impersonator Fregoli is presented to the public.

Debut of the Spanish dramatic troupe which features Luisa Segovia.

1902

María Guerrero and Fernando Díaz de Mendoza with their dramatic company.

The Ministry of Public Education and Fine Arts awards a stipend to Manuela Eugenia Torres so that she may study dramatic arts with María Guerrero.

On July 23 Gerardo López del Castillo, dean of Mexican actors, dies.

Concerts by the pianist Artemisa Elizondo.

1903

The soprano Amalia de Roma performs.

At the Teatro Arbeu the opera company featuring Luisa Tetrazzini, Virgilo Bellati, Giulio Rossi, María Grisi, etc., has its debut. This company performs *Werther* and *Haensel and Gretel* in Mexico.

1904

Debut of the dramatic company of Emilio Thuillier, with Mercedes Díaz Gambadella, Ana Mollar Ferri and María Victorero in the work *From Bad Stock,* by Echegaray.

Debut of the French opera and operetta company of Paule Prévost and N. Lacane at the Teatro Renacimiento.

Teresa Mariani, Vittorio Zampieri, Emma Ricardini, Césare Zopetti, Marinela Bragaglia, etc., appear at the Teatro Arbeu.

The one hundredth performance of *Chin Chun Chan,* by Rafael Medina, José F. Elizondo and Maestro Luis G. Jordá, is celebrated at the Teatro Principal with María Luisa Label, Francisco Gavilanes, Consuela Vivanco, Eduardo Arozamena, Esperanza Iris, Emilia Plaza, Pilar Leredo, Manuel Noriega, etc., participating.

At the Teatro Hidalgo the Spanish dramatic actress Elisa de la Maza performs.

At the Teatro Arbeu the Italian opera company with Luisa Tetrazzini, Livia Berlendi and others is featured.

1905

Dramatic company of Italia Vitaliani.

Scognamiglio Italian operetta company, with Linda Gattini, Anetta Fontana and others.

Coronation of the dramatist José Peón y Contreras.

Dramatic company of Virginia Reiter, with Piperno and Luigi Carini.

Dramatic company of Consuela López de Solano, with the lead actor Teissier.

Italian ballet company with Carmesi and Ida Zori, among others. Production of the ballet *Excelsior.*

María Barrientos arrives.

The American Dramatic Company, in which Beryl Hope, Lottie Alter, Edwin Mordaunt, Grace Atwell, Louis Mackintosh, Osward Bowles and Robert Rogers are featured, appears at the Teatro Renacimiento.

Teatro Arbeu. Italian opera company, with Luisa Tetrazzini, Carlos Barrera, Ester Adalberto, Guermi and the baritone Rebonato.

1906

Teatro Hidalgo. Dramatic company of Felipe de J. Haro.

María Reig, ingenue of the Virginia Fábregas Company, dies in Chihuahua at the hands of Manuel Algara.

Rosalía Chalía devotes herself to the *género chico.*

Concerts by the fourteen year old violinist Florisel von Reuter.

Concerts by the Mexican singer Elena Marín.

The motion picture appears for the first time.

Dramatic company of Francisco Fuentes, with Consuelo Abad.

Lombardi opera company. (*Germania,* by Franchetti, *Chopin* and *Iris,* by Mascagni.)

Success of *The Green Wave* and *The Cup of Tea* at the Teatro Principal.

At the Teatro Hidalgo, dramatic company of María Luisa Villegas and Leopoldina Galza.

Death of Constantino Cires Sánchez.

Opera company of Aldo Barrilli, with Poli Randaccio, Gisella Ferrari, Virginia Guerrerini, Giuseppina Picoletti, Alfredo Cecchi, Angel Pintucci, Coletti and others.

Death of the theatrical actor Alfredo Chavero.

Death of the dramatist Manuel José Othón (December 2).

Construction is begun on the Teatro Lírico.

1907

Dramatic company of Ermette Novelli, with Olga Giamini.

The singer Rosalía Chalía has the tombstone of Angela Peralta repaired and adorned at her own expense.

The dramatist and poet José Peón y Contereas dies.

American operetta company with Edna Purdyg, Alice Roberts and Paulina Earlenite (production of *Florodora*).

The pianist Ana María Charles and the singer Fanny Anitúa begin to perform.

(First automobile races.)

Teatro Arbeu. The Fuentes-Arévalo dramatic company performs *Madame Sans-Gene,* previously introduced by Teresa Mariani.

Concerts by the Brussels Quartet.

Opening of the Teatro Lírico.

Concerts by the pianist Jessie Shay.

Teatro Arbeu. Opera company with Matilde de Lerma and others.

The soprano María Conesa has her debut on November 1.

Return of María Guerrero and Fernando Díaz de Mendoza.

The Mexican composer Ricardo Castro dies (November 20).

Concerts by the pianist José Hoffman.

Concerts by the Mexican pianist Alberto Villaseñor.

The French singer Emma Calvé appears.

1908

Concerts by the violinist Renée Chemet.

Teatro V. Fábregas. Opera with Mme Giudice, Mme Monte Bruner, etc.

Teatro Arbeu — May 10 —. Concerts by the violinist Fritz Kreisler.

Concerts by the trio composed of María Luisa Degobis, Emeric Stefaniai and Cesare Barisson.

French drama company with Mlle Rhéa, Jane Kosta, etc.

Concerts by the violinist Willy Burmester.

The Palmes Academiques are presented to the Mexican actress Virginia Fábregas.

A Mexican opera company is formed with Adriana Delgado, Flora Arroyo, Sofía Camacho, María de Jesús Magaña de López, José Torres Ovando, Julio Vilderique.

Teatro Principal. Operetta and *zarzuela* troupe with Sara López, Amparo Romo, Amparo Pozuelo, Luis Morón and Julia Fons.

The Mexican singers María Luisa Escobar and Manuel Romero Malpica begin to appear in the opera and the actor Ricardo Mutio performs along with Virginia Fábregas in *The Victim,* by Gaston Dévore.

Soledad Goyzueta performs at the Orrin Amphitheater.

Pastora Imperio has her debut at the Teatro Principal.

Dramatic company of Enrique Borrás.

Debut of the dramatic troupe of Tina di Lorenzo with *The Thief.*

1909

Concerts by Joseph Hofmann.

The Teatro Lírico becomes the "Folies Bergères."

Concerts by Josef Lhévinne.

Death of the Spanish actor Leopoldo Burón.

First visit by Mimí Aguglia, with Atilio Rapisarda and his sisters Teresa and Sara Aguglia (*The Daughter of Iorio, Zazá, Sonciura*).

Concerts by the cellist Joseph Malkin who, along with Schoer, Mircy and Daucher, is a member of the Brussels Quartet.

Concerts by the pianist Adela Verne at the Metropolitan Academy.

Emilio Thuillier returns with Rosario Pino in his troupe. (*The Bonds of Interest.*)

A company composed of students from the Conservatory: Rosita Arriaga, Carlos Solórzano and Manuel de la Bandera, performs briefly at the Teatro Arbeu.

Opening of the Teatro Rosa Fuertes (formerly the Apolo), on Mosqueta Street, with a company in which Elena de la Llata, Julia Abad, María Winol, Carmen Beltrán, etc., perform. It is of no consequence.

1910

Ruggero Ruggeri and Lyda Borelli come to Mexico, bringing to the stage works of Ibsen, Rostand, Giacosa, and *Salomé,* by Oscar Wilde.

Concerts by Josef Lhévinne.

Virginia Fábregas appears for a run at her theater together with Julio Taboada.

Debut of the dancer Lydia de Rostow together with the Mexican Josefina, the Spaniard Sacramento and the Frenchwoman Gyka.

The poet Juan de Dios Peza dies on May 15.

Additional concerts by the American pianist Olga Steeb.

Opera company with María Pozzi and the baritone Angelini, Jane Noria, Leonip Samoiloff (Rabinoff Enterprises).

Teatro Arbeu. The Sagí-Barba Company (*The Princess of the Dollar,* by Leo Fall; *The Merry Widow,* by Lehar; *The King who went mad,* etc.) with Luisa Vela and others.

Teatro Colón. Consuelo Abad.

1911

Teatro Arbeu. Operetta company of Esperanza Iris, with Josefina Peral.

New production with Mimí Aguglia (*The Dinners of Derision,* by Sem Benelli, etc.). Dante Cappelli arrived with her.

Concerts by the pianist Arthur Friedheim.

Ricardo Bell dies in New York City.

Company of Juan Balaguer and Conchita Catalá.

Esther Groizard and Enrique Tovar Avalos present themselves at the declamation competition held at the Conservatory.

Consuelo Escobar receives a first prize in the third year singing class.

Virginia Macías, María Romero, Martínez Vieyra and Angel Esquivel, youthful beginners, produce *La Bohème* at the Teatro Colón.

Teatro Arbeu. Company of Dante Cappelli and Celeste Aída Zanchi.

Pantomine troupe of Molasso with Eugenia Fougère and Esther Scozzi.

Concerts by the French pianist Julia Bal.

Concerts by the German tenor Ludwig Hers.

Teatro Arbeu. Opera company with Esperanza Montero del Collado, Regina Viccarino, Eugenio Battain, Giuseppe Picco, Anna Ferry, José Torres Ovando.

Among the Tenorios of this year can be counted that of Mario Vittoria at the Arbeu and that of Mutio at the Colón.

Opera company of M. Masson, with Cecilia Tomanti Zavasky and Rodolfo Amadi. Teatro Colón.

1912

María Conesa is proclaimed Queen of the *género chico*.

Concerts by the Hungarian pianist Yolanda Méroe.

Teatro Arbeu. Mexican dramatic group of Manuela Eugenia Torres. Appears later at the Teatro Mexicano.

The dramatic company of Miguel Muñoz produces *The Tribune*, by Bourget. Olga van Camps, Julio Soto, Virginia Nevares and others appear with it. (*The Claw, Life is a Dream, In Flanders the Sun has Set, Don Alvaro or the Force of Destiny,* et cétera.)

Teatro Arbeu. The company of Esperanza Iris produces *The Count of Luxembourg, Spring Breezes, The Merry Widow, The Chaste Susana, Viennese Blood, The Chocolate Soldier,* with libretto by Nan de Allariz — who is in Mexico City —, *John the Second, The Princess of the Balkans, The Geisha,* by Silver Jones, *The Fourth Dimension,* etc. Josefina Peral, Juan Palmer and others perform there.

The French soprano Yvonne de Treville arrives.

The Peruvian poet José Santos Chocano arrives in Mexico.

The writer Justo Sierra dies in Madrid.

As a result of the dismissal of Arcaraz Enterprises, the Teatro Principal is shut down after twenty years of the *género chico*.

Debut of Mimí Derba at the Teatro Lírico.

Teatro Principal: "Florodoras" Sextet.

The Italian opera company featuring Alessandro Bonci, Ester Toninello, Francesco Zani, Fanny Antúa, la Galimbert, Irma Dalossy, Salvatore Sciarreti, Agnese Hanick, Roberto Corruchini, etc., arrives.

1913

Teatro Colón, Presentation of the company of Alfredo Sainati and Bella Starace with works from the Adult Puppet Theater, a genre which they are said to have created.

Death of the composer Ernesto Elorduy.

Tragic death of the baritone Enrique Labrada.

Teatro Arbeu. Spanish dramatic company of Enrique Borrás.

Teatro Principal. Gattini-Angelini opera company.

Death of the tenor José Vigil y Robles.

Teatro Colón. Detective drama company of Ramón Carralt (*Nick Carter, Arsène Lupin, The Mystery of the Yellow Room,* etc.)

Death of the actor Enrique Quijada.

Alfredo Gómez (de la Vega), "notable orator," gives a literary recital.

Teatro Arbeu. Mexican opera company with María de la Fraga, Adriana Delgado, Manuel Mendoza López, Angel Esquivel, Vilderique, Anaya, Panciera and others.

Teatro Hidalgo. Mexican opera company with Ada Navarrete, María M. de la Fraga, Soledad Abaunza, M. L. Espinosa, Edmundo Anaya and F. Loyo.

The actor Francisco Cardona dies.

Alberto Michel wins a first prize in the *zarzuela* contest sponsored by the Mexican Theatrical Company.

1914

Presentation by the actress Dora Vila of *The Passion Flower* at the Acacia.

Teatro Arbeu. Operetta Company of Carmen Caussade.

Teatro Ideal. After Easter, a dramatic company composed of Dora Vila, Elisa Asperó, Concepción Adzuar, Clara Martínez, Paz Villegas, Lolita Asperó, Magdalene Navarro, Socorro Astol, Concepción Sotomayor, Ana Carrillo, etc., has its debut.

Teatro Mexicano. Idem: Matilde Cires Sánchez, Emilia del Castillo, Prudencia Grifell, Mercedes Navarro, Consuelo Segarra, Angélica Méndez, Emilia Otazo.

Teatro Principal. A género chico company featuring María Caballé, Mimí Derba, Clementina Morín and Carmen Caussade has its debut after Easter.

Teatro Colón. Idem: an operetta company with María de los Angeles García Blanco, Soledad Alvarez, Adelina Iris, Guadalupe Rodrigo.

The writer Rafael Delgado dies.

Company of Romualdo Tirado at the Welton Amphitheater.

Mimí Derba has her debut in the play at the Teatro Mexicano (*Polichinela's Secret*).

Teatro Colón. Dramatic company of Miguel Muñoz with María Luisa Villegas, Dora Vila, etc.

Alfredo Gómez de la Vega "recites successfully at the Ateneo of Madrid."

Teatro Hidalgo. Opera company with Esquivel, Mendoza and Serazzi.

Death of the actress Teresa Mariani.

Teatro Arbeu. Opera company of Sigaldi.

1915

Opening of the Teatro Ruiz de Alarcón by the dramatic company of Ricardo Mutio and Dora Vila.

Teatro Arbeu. Opera company with María Teresa Santillán, Carlos Mejía, Eduardo Lejarazu, Josefina Llaca, María Romero, Saldaña, Carmen García Cornejo, etc.

Teatro Lírico. Opera company with María Cristina Islas, Rodolfo Navarrete, Mendoza López, Bice Pizzorni Gini, etc.

Recitals by the pianist Manuel Barajas.

1916

Concerts by Luis Alfonso Marrón.

Strike by unionized actors. Formation of a union for artists.

Teatro Arbeu. Company for the Encouragement of Opera of Maestro Pierson with Josefina Llaca, etc.

Guadalupe Rivas Cacho and Celia Bonoris at the Teatro Lírico.

Death of the actress María Luisa Villegas.

1917

Teatro Mexicano. The ingenue María Teresa Montoya is presented.

María Conesa, who had her debut in 1907 (November 1), is married and announces her retirement from the stage.

The Spanish poet Salvador Rueda comes to Mexico.

Showing of the film *Light,* by Emma Padilla. First national production in this genre.

Visit by the Argentine journalist and writer Manuel Ugarte.

Visit by the Spanish poet Francisco Villaespesa.

Organization of Aztec Films.

The dancer Antonia Mercé de Paz, "La Argentina," is presented.

Teatro Arbeu. Opera company with Giovanni Zenatello, Rosa Raisa, Giacomo Rimini, Esther Ferralini, Andrea de Segurola, Ricardo Stracciari, Maggie Teyte, Millo Picco, María Gay, Virgilio Lazzari, Ana Fitziu, Vicente Baristie, Tamiki Miura, Leone Zinovieff, Edith Mason, Giorgio Polacco.

María Conesa returns to the theater.

Concerts by the pianist Rosa Renard.

1918

Arrival of the Spanish dancer Tórtola Valencia.

Concerts by the Argentine violinist Dalmau at the Fábregas.

Teatro Colón. Dramatic company directed by Francisco Villaespesa. (*The Cardinal's Supper,* by Julio Dantás, performed by Villaespesa, Manuel Sierra Méndez and Eduardo Gómez Haro; *Christmas Ballad,* by J. Jiménez Rueda, *Hernán Cortés,* by Villaespesa.)

Presentation of the Italian impersonator Bernardi.

Teatro Arbeu. Presentation of the ballerina Norka Rouskaya.

Teatro Virginia Fábregas. Ballet company with María Léger and Margot Ladd (*The Ebony Horse, Coppelia.*)

The little violinist Celia Treviño appears.

Resurgence of the Company for the Encouragement of Opera, with María Romero, Consuelo Calvera, Josefina Llaca, Angel Esquivel, Carlos Mejía, Luis de Ibargüen, Ernesto Rubio, Diana Martínez Milícua, Saldaña, etc.

Opening of the Teatro Esperanza Iris on May 21.

Presentation of the Pro-Arte Company with Rosita Zotti and María Luisa Escobar de Rocabruna.

Concerts by the French pianist Maurice Dumesnil.

Presentation of Armanda Chirot, Rosa Basurto, Miguel Angel Ortiz, Luis Díaz de León and Luis García Carrillo, students at the Conservatory, in *The Way to Perfection,* by Julio Jiménez Rueda, *The Cardinals' Supper* and *Roses All Year Long,* by Julio Dantás.

Teatro Iris. Velasco-Velarde Company, with Consuelo Mayendía and the dancer Violeta Fernández, etc.

In trials at the Conservatory, directed by J. Jiménez Rueda, Armanda Chirot, Angela Rebolledo, Mercedes Ferriz, Emilio Gandarilla, L. García Carrillo, Ernesto Urtusástegui, etc., in *Marianela,* by Benito Pérez Galdós, are presented. Among students at the Conservatory also are Isaura Cano, Elvira Cano, Emma Siliceo, Clara Esther Tapia, etc.

1919

Return of the dancer Tórtola Valencia.

Concerts by the cellist Pablo Casals.

January 11. Ana Pavlova has her debut with Wlasta Maslova, Hilda Butzova, Alexander Volinine, Ivan Glustin, etc.

Quinito Valverde dies.

Teatro Arbeu. Porredón drama company.

Teatro Iris. Opera company directed by G. Polacco, with Rosa Raisa, Alessandro Dolci, Edith Mason, Consuelo Escobar, Tita Ruggo, Virgilo Lazzari, Gabriela Besanzoni and the dancers Wlasta Maslova, Carmen Galé and Wladimer Worontzoff.

The poet Amado Nervo dies in Montevideo.

Concerts by the pianist Arthur Rubinstein.

The tenor Enrico Caruso enters the field of opera.

The Enemy, by Darío Nicodemi, is performed by Beatriz Eldridge, Isaura Cano and Gustavo Curiel, students at the Conservatory.

The Spanish tenor Florencio Costantino goes insane after losing his voice and dies in Mexico.

1920

Debut of the Bracale Opera company with Carmen Melis, etc.

Concerts by the Symphonic Orchestra under the direction of Maestro Julián Carrillo.

Visit by the Spanish writer Vicente Blasco Ibáñez.

Return of the dramatic company of Ramón Caralt.

The dancer Antonia Mercé, "La Argentina," returns.

At a function honoring Federico Gamboa, Enrique Tovar Avalos, Elena Sánchez Valenzuela and Adela Maza, all students at the Conservatory, perform one of his works.

Performances by the Virginia Fábregas company.

Spanish operetta company of Maestro Manuel Penella.

Valle-Scillag operetta company, with Stefi Scillag, at the Teatro Arbeu.

Opera company of Com. Arturo Baralta with the Spanish soprano Mercedes Capsir.

1921

Arrival of the actor Rafael Arcos.

Eugenia Zuffoli performs at the Iris.

Concerts by the pianist Josef Lhévinne.

Showing of the motion picture "Open Wings," with Carmen Bonifant, Luis Ross, Jeska Burnett, Carrillo de Albornoz and others.

The actress and popular singer María Tubau returns.

Presentation of the actress Margarita Xirgú.

The poet Ramón López Velarde dies.

Concert by the pianist Leopold Godowski.

Enrico Caruso dies.

Teatro Iris. Jack Mason Follies.

Visit by the Spanish poet Ramón María del Valle-Inclán.

Centenary opera company with Fernando Doría, Ofelia Nieto, Tito Schipa, Alicia Haester, Virgilio Lazzari, Fanny Anitúa, Claudia Muzzio, Angeles Ottein, etc.

Teatro Arbeu. Centenary Ballet, with Cristina Pereda, etcetera.

1922

Presentation of the Argentine actress Camila Quiroga with her dramatic company.

Dramatic company of Felipe Sassone and María Palov.

Presentation of the Spanish actress Gloria Torrea.

Formalization of the union of artists which had failed previously.

Concerts by Bavagnoli.

Recognition of the union by the Teatro Principal, Teatro Lírico and Teatro Hidalgo.

Concerts by the pianist Ignaz Friedman.

Margarita Xirgú and her company at the Arbeu.

Margarita Xirgú's first attempt at open-air theater at the Chapultepec Rotunda with *Electra,* by Hugo von Hoffmannsthal.

Presentation of the Spanish actor Ernesto Vilches and his wife Irene López de Heredia. (Vilches worked previously with Balaguer and with Virginia Fábregas.)

The Mexican Regional Theater begins at San Juan Teotihuacán with *The Crossing,* by Rafael M. Saavedra.

Presentation of the Pavley-Oukrainsky Russian ballet company.

Teatro Arbeu. Italian dramatic company with Mimí Aguglia and Giovanni Grasso.

Visit by the Chilean poetess Gabriela Mistral.

Run of Mexican plays as the Teatro de la Comedia (Lírico).

The actress María Teresa Montoya returns.

Recital by the pianist María Carreras.

The Spanish tenor Miguel Fleta performs in the opera.

Presentation of the Ukrainian Choruses of Maestro Alexander Koshetz.

1923

The actress Virginia Fábregas returns.

Presentation of the dramatic company of Jacinto Benavente, with Lola Membrives as leading lady.

Armen Ohanian, Persian dancer.

French drama company of Pierre Maguier, with Juliette Clarel, Blanche Toutain, etc.

First National Congress of Artists and Writers.

Concerts by the pianist Josef Lhévinne.

Tórtola Valencia returns.

Presentation of the Spanish guitarist Andrés Segovia.

Teatro Municipal (Virginia Fábregas. María Teresa Montoya company.)

Teatro Iris. Russian opera company (*Boris Godounov,* etc.)

The artist Soledad Goyzueta dies.

The UDAD is formed. (Union of Dramatic Writers.)

Appearance of the soprano Delia Magaña.

Alfredo Gómez de la Vega triumphs in the Spanish theater.

Presentation of the popular singer Conchita Piquer.

The dramatist Marcelino Dávalos dies on September 14.

Juan Vicente Gómez, President of the Republic of Venezuela, opposes, because of the difficulties which have emerged between the two nations, the disembarkation of the Wimer-Sánchez revue troupe.

The Vittone-Pomar Argentine company, with Olinda Bozán, María Esther Pomar, Segundo Pomar, etc. (First *género chico* company of that nationality to come to Mexico.)

Presentation of Berta Singerman, Argentine reciter.

Synthetic Theater of Rafael M. Saavedra, Carlos González and Francisco Domínguez.

1924

Founding of the Poets, Essayists and Novelists Club. (P.E.N. Club).

Theater of the Bat begun by Carlos González, Luis Quintilla and Francisco Domínguez.

Teatro Iris. An opera company with María Cantoni and the tenor Alvarez.

Visit by the Colombian writer José María Vargas Vila.

Signing of the dramatic-literary properties treaty with Spain.

Opening of the Teatro Regis with the presentation of the popular singer Teresita Zazá.

María Tubau has difficulties with the Union of Artists.

The actor Fernando Soler emerges at the Teatro Ideal with a company in which Sagra del Río figures as the leading lady.

Teatro Regis. Presentation of the Cossacks from Kubán.

Book Fair at the Palacio de Minería.

1925

Teatro Fábregas. Chamber opera with Angeles Ottein, the Belgian baritone Armand Crabbé and Carlos del Pozo.

Teatro Regis. Pavley-Oukrainsky.

Teatro Iris. Presentation of the fifth or sixth rate spectacle called "Ba-Ta-clan," by Mne Rasimi.

Visit by the writers Eduardo Zamacois and Joaquín Belda.

The Spanish actress and writer María Álvarez de Burgos appears unsuccessfully in vaudeville together with the Mexican actor Luis G. Barreiro.

Olimpia Cinema. Ottein-Crabbé opera company.

Concerts by the pianist Alexander Brailowsky. Teatro Regis.

The dancer Ana Pavlowa appears again with her ballet company in which the dancer Novikoff figures.

Dramatic company of María Fernanda Ladrón de Guevara and Rafael Rivelles. Teatro Regis.

Visit by the Argentine writer Alejandro Sux.

The Mexican actress Dora Vila, who worked beside Alfredo Gómez de la Vega, dies on July 25 in Spain.

Lupe Rivas Cacho visits Spain and South America.

Presentation of the dancer Enid Romany.

Dramatic contest of *El Universal Ilustrado*. (First prize awarded to V. M. Díez Barroso for *Control Yourself*.)

1926

January. Presentation by the Mexican reciter Adela Formoso.

Spanish dramatic company of the actress María Arcos at the Teatro Fábregas.

Virginia Fábregas returns to the country.

Performance by the Ike Rose performing dwarfs at the Teatro Iris.

Spanish dramatic company of the actor Ricardo Calvo. (Iris.)

French dramatic company of Porte Saint-Martin, headed by the actress Gabrielle Dorziat, at the Teatro Arbeu.

The little Hispano-Argentine actor Narcisín, 13 years of age, is at the Teatro Iris.

Presentation of the Mexican pianist Angélica Morales.

Ramón Caralt returns bringing Raimunda Gaspar as leading lady.

Run by the Group of Seven at the Teatro Fábregas (*A Farce,* by V. M. Díez Barroso, etc.).

Presentation by the Mexican reciter Isabella Corona.

Dramatic company of Ernesto Vilches and Irene López de Heredia.

The Christ of Gold, Mexican motion picture by Otilia Zambrano, Fanny Schiller, Luis Márquez, etc.

The actor Alfredo Gómez de la Vega returns to Mexico.

Sugrañes Revue Company at the Teatro Iris.

Concerts by the guitarist Francisco Callejas.

The Mexican dancer Celia Pérez dies on December 6 in Tocornal, Chile.

1927

Vittanova Argentine troupe.

Miguel Ángel Ferriz returns to Mexico after working with María Guerrero and Fernando Díaz de Mendoza.

Teatro Iris. Company of performing dogs.

María Guerrero and Fernando Díaz de Mendoza return.

Archduchess Carlota Amalia, ex-Empress of Mexico, dies in Belgium on January 19.

Mimí Aguglia begins to perform in Spanish with Alfredo Gómez de la Vega.

Virginia Fábregas goes to Los Angeles.

The soprano Lupe Vélez departs for Los Angeles where she has been given a contract to make motion pictures.

Arrival of the aviator Charles A. Lindbergh.

Recitals by the Cherniavsky Trio at the Teatro Arbeu.

Teatro Regis. Presentation of the company of the Spanish dramatist Gregorio Martínez Sierra, with Catalina Bárcena as leading lady.

Concerts by the violinist Jascha Heifetz at the Teatro Arbeu and the Iris.

1928

The Teatro de Ulises opens.

Visit by the French aviators Dieudonné Costes and Joseph Lebrix.

The Camila Quiroga company returns.

Teatro Regis. Dramatic company of María Herrero.

Presentation of the company of Jesús Tordesillas.

The Spanish actor Jaime Borrás has his debut at the Teatro Fábregas.

Lupita Rovar and the soprano Delia Magaña depart for Los Angeles, California, after receiving prizes in a motion picture contest.

Presentation in the opera of the tenor Dr. Alfonso Ortiz Tirado.

1929

Beginning of the Public Entertainment for the Federal District, and other theatrical activities, under the direction of the writer

Amalia G. C. de Castillo Ledón, including the Teatro del Periquillo founded by Bernardo Ortiz de Montellano, Julio Castellanos and the Guerrero brothers.

Concerts by the Argentine pianist Hector Ruiz Díaz.

A Mexican play is performed at the Teatro Regis and afterward at the Ideal.

Virginia Fábregas returns to Mexico.

1930

Theatrical run of Alfredo Gómez de la Vega at the Teatro Arbeu (*The Thought, Topaze,* by Marcel Pagnol; *Maya,* by Simón Gantillon; *The Man Who Met Himself,* etc.).

Concerts by the Argentine pianist Hector Ruiz Díaz.

Privé Opera from Paris at the Teatro Iris.

Teatro Iris. Sugrañes Revue Company.

Teatro Virginia Fábregas. Spanish dramatic company of Pepita Díaz and Santiago Artigas. (*A Doll's House, Crossed Lives,* by Benavente, *The White Monk,* by Marquina, etc.

Teatro Fábregas. Rambal company.

1931

January 22. Anna Pavlova, exponent of beauty, dies in The Hague.

January 29. The dramatist and critic José Joaquín Gamboa dies.

March 1. Fire at the Teatro Principal.

Visit by the Spanish raconteur Federico García Sánchez.

Visit by the Spanish writer José María Salaverría.

Performance by Leopold Stokowski, conductor of the Philadelphia Symphony Orchestra, directing the Symphony Orchestra of Mexico.

Teatro Fábregas. Theatrical run featuring the actress María Teresa Montoya.

Presentation of the Mexican dancer Pedro Rubín.

Tribute in memory of José Joaquín Gamboa with the performance of his work *Spirits*.

Visit by the movie director Eisenstein.

The actress Virginia Fábregas returns.

June. Founding of the "Friends of the Mexican Theater" Society.

Inauguration of the Teatro Orientación by the Department of Fine Arts of the Secretariat of Public Education.

Theatrical run of Virginia Fábregas at her theater with Mexican and foreign works. Among the latter are *Doubt,* by Adolfo Fernández Bustamante, *The Miracle of Tepeyac,* by Father Heredia, etc.

Readings of works at the "Friends of the Mexican Theater" Society by A Granja Irigoyen, Mauricio Magdaleno, Juan Bustillo Oro, María Luisa Ocampo, Francisco Monterde, R. Navarrete, Rodolfo Usigli, A. Fernández Bustamante, Ernesto Lozano García, Julio Jiménez Rueda, V. M. Díez Barroso, Fernando Mota and Antonio Helú.

1932

Recital of Mexican dances by the ballerina Yol-Izma, at the Teatro Orientación.

Concerts by the pianist Ignaz Friedman.

February 12, The season of the Teatro de Ahora, of Juan Bustillo Oro and Mauricio Magdaleno (*Emiliano Zapata, Shark, Pánuco 137, Those Who Return*) begins at the Teatro Hidalgo. Ricardo Mutio, Alberto Galán, Frausto, Socorro Astol, Lidia Franco, E. Romero and others are featured in the cast.

March 31. The symphony-ballet *H. P.,* by the Mexican composer Carlos Chávez, is performed by the Philadelphia Symphony Orchestra conducted by Leopold Stokowski. Sets are by Diego Rivera. Story and arrangement are by Chávez, Rivera and Frances Flynn Paine; choreography is under the direction of Catherine Littlefield.

Concerts by the French cellist Lucienne Radisse.

The Virginia Fábregas company produces *Juárez and Maximilian,* by the Austrian Franz Werfel, translated by Enrique Jiménez Domínguez.

April 30. The dramatist Carlos Díaz Dufoo, Jr., dies in Atzcapotzalco.

Concerts by the Russian singer Sonia Verbitzky.

Theatrical productions by Ernesto Vilches at the Teatro Arbeu and the Teatro Fábregas with María Conesa, Virginia Zurí, Carlos Orellana, René Cardona, etc.

Lectures by the humorist and dramatist José F. Elizondo (Pepe Nava).

June 16. Founding of the Cine-Club of Mexico.

Presentation of the Alegría and Enhart company at the Teatro Politeama.

June 17. Presentation at the Teatro Ideal of the María Guerrero-Fernando Díaz de Mendoza company with *The Gardener's Dog,* by Lope de Vega, arranged by Antonio and Manuel Machado.

June 25. The Teatro Lírico changes its name to "The Palace of Laughter," and Isabel and Ana Blanch, Matilde Corell, Eduardo Vivas, Carlos Orellana, José Luis Jiménez, Mario Martínez Casado, etc., perform there.

Visit by the French novelist Marc Chadourne.

The symphonic poem Cuauhtémoc, by the Mexican composer José Rolón, is performed by the Berliner Funkorchester conducted by Bruno Seidler-Winkler.

July 1, *The Itchy Parrot,* a revue by Juan Bustillo Oro and Mauricio Magdaleno, is produced at the Teatro Esperanza Iris by the Roberto Soto company.

July 7. Institution of the Municipal Prize by the Central Department of the Federal District. (One thousand pesos to the best Mexican play performed every three months.)

July 15. The Central Department institutes another prize of one thousand pesos for the best Mexican motion picture which is shown every three months.

I extend the most profound appreciation to Luis González Obregón, Francisco Monterde and Felipe Teixidor as well as to the other persons who favorably received the idea for this book and furnished information without which I would have been unable to complete it.

R. U.

GUIDE TO QUOTATIONS AND BIBLIOGRAPHY

Page

BIBLIOGRAPHY

Abreu Gómez, Ermilo. "Un aspecto del Teatro Romántico. Peón y Contreras." In journal *Contemporáneos,* Mexico City. No. 30-31, Nov.-Dec., 1930.

———. "Vida y obra de Sor Juana." In journal *Contemporáneos,* Mexico City. No. 40-41, Sept.-Oct., 1931.

Acosta, Father José de. *Historia Natural y Moral de las Indias.* Pantaleón Aznar, publisher. Madrid. MDCCXCII. (National Library of Mexico.)

Actas de Cabildo de la Ciudad de México. (Central Department of the Federal District.)

Antología del Centenario. Compiled under the direction of Justo Sierra by Luis G. Urbina, Pedro Henríquez Ureña and Nicolás Rangel. Mexico City. Manuel León Sánchez, printer. 1910.

Barrera, Carlos. "Lo nacional en el Teatro." *El Universal Ilustrado.* Mexico City. August 8, 1929.

Benavente, Fr. Toribio de (Motolinia). *Historia de los Indios de Nueva España.* Barcelona, 1914. (National Library of Mexico).

Bernard Shaw, George. *La Dama Morena de los Sonetos.* Trans. by Julio Broutá. M. Aguilar, Publisher. Madrid.

Calderón de la Barca, Pedro. *Teatro.* Prologue by Justo Gómez Ocerin. Editorial Calleja. Madrid, 1920.

Campos, Rubén M. *El Folklore Musical de las Ciudades*. Publications of the Secretaría de Educación Pública. Mexico City, 1930. (National Museum of Mexico.)

Castañeda, C. E. "Descripción de las Obras de Cristóbal Gutiérrez de Luna." *Revista Mexicana de Estudios Históricos*. Volume II, no. 5. Mexico City, 1931. (National Library of Mexico.)

Castillo Ledón, Luis. "Los Mexicanos Autores de Operas." *Anales del Museo Nacional de Arqueología, Historia y Etnología*. Volume II, Mexico City, 1910. (National Library of Mexico.)

————. *Vida de Miguel Hidalgo y Costilla* (in preparation).

Castro Santa-Anna, José Manuel. *Diario de Sucesos Notables*. Mexico, 1854. Juan R. Navarro, printer.

Codex Borbonicus. Paris. Ernest Leroux, Editeur. 1899. (National Library of Mexico.)

Códice Ramírez. Manuscript of the sixteenth century. José M. Vigil, Publisher. Mexico City. Printing and lithography by Ireneo Paz (Biblioteca Mexicana) 1878. (National Museum of Mexico).

Chávez, Ezequiel A. *Sor Juana Inés de la Cruz*. Editorial Araluce. Barcelona, 1931 (National Library of Mexico.)

Del Paso y Troncoso, Francisco. *Diversos autos traducidos del mexicano*. (National Museum of Mexico.)

Díaz del Castillo, Bernal. *Historia Verdadera de la Conquista de la Nueva España*. Only edition according to autograph manuscript. Genaro García published it. Printing Office of the Secretaría de Fomento. Mexico City, 1904 (National Library of Mexico.)

Diccionario de Geografía, Historia y Bibliografía Mexicanas. Alberto Leduc, Dr. Luis Lara Pardo and Carlos Roumagnac. Librería Vda. de C. Bouret. 1910.

Diccionario Universal de Historia y Geografía. Volume V. "Mexico." Manuel Orozco y Berra. Mexico City, 1854. (National Library of Mexico.)

Documentos para la Historia de Mexico. National Library, Mss.

Durán, Dr. Diego. *Historia de las Indias de Nueva España y Islas de Tierra Firme*. José F. Ramírez has published it with an *Atlas de Estampas, Notas e Ilustraciones*. Two volumes. Mexico City. J. M. Andrade and F. Escalante, Printers. Bajos de San Agustín No. 1, 1867 (National Museum of Mexico.)

Efemérides a cargo de Ignacio Cornejo. "El Renacimiento." Volume I. Mexico City, 1869. (National Library of Mexico.)

Fülop-Miller, R. and J. Gregor. *El Teatro Ruso*. Gustavo Gili, Publisher. Barcelona.

García Cubas, Antonio. *El Libro de mis Recuerdos*. Mexico City, 1904. Arturo García Cubas, Hnos. Sucrs., Printers. (National Library of Mexico.)

García, Genaro. *Documentos para la Historia de México*. Volume XII. Mexico City, 1907. (National Library of Mexico.)

García Icazbalceta, Joaquín. *Bibliografía Mexicana del siglo XVI*. Mexico City, 1886. (National Library of Mexico.)

González de Eslava, Presbyter Fernán. *Coloquios Espirituales y Sacramentales y Poesías Sagradas*. Prologue by Joaquín García Icazbalceta. Mexico City, 1877. (National Library of Mexico.)

González Obregón, Luis. *México Viejo*. Librería Vda. de Ch. Bouret. Paris-Mexico City, 1900. (National Library of Mexico.)

180 BIBLIOGRAPHY

González Peña, Carlos. *Historia de la Literatura Mexicana*. Publication of the Secretaría de Educación Pública. Mexico City, 1928.

Guijo, Gregorio Martín de. *Diario de Sucesos Notables*. Mexico City, 1853. Juan R. Navarro, Printer. (National Library of Mexico.)

Henríquez Ureña, Pedro. *Seis Ensayos en Busca de Nuestra Expresión*. Editorial B.A.B.E.L., Buenos Aires.

Larousse XXe Siècle. Librairie Larousse. Paris. (Alliance Française de Mexico.)

Mañón, Manuel. *Historia del Teatro Principal* (in preparation).

Monterde, Francisco. *Bibliografía del Teatro en México* (in preparation).

Nietzsche, Friederich. *El Crepúsculo de los Ídolos*. Trans. J. E. de Muñagorri. Rafael Caro Raggio, Publisher, Madrid.

Olavarría y Ferrari, Enrique de. *Reseña Histórica del Teatro en México*. Mexico City, 1895. "La Europea." (National Library of Mexico.)

Peón y Contreras, José. *Obras Dramáticas*. With a biographical segment by V. Agüeros. Biblioteca de Autores Mexicanos. V. Agüeros, Printer. Mexico City, 1896.

Peñafiel, Dr. Antonio. *Indumentaria Antigua, Armas, Vestidos Guerreros y Civiles de los Antiguos Mexicanos*. Mexico City. Printing Office of the Secretaría de Fomento. Mexico City, 1903.

Piscator, Erwin. *El Teatro Político*. Trans. Salvador Vila. Editorial Cenit. Madrid.

Robles, Antonio de. *Diario de Sucesos Notables*. Mexico City, 1853. Juan R. Navarro, Printer. (National Library of Mexico.)

Toussaint, Manuel. "Documentos para la Historia del Teatro en México." *In Libros, Revista Mensual de Bibliografía*. Volume I, no. 4. Mexico City. June, 1931. (National Library of Mexico.)

Valle-Arizpe, Artemio de. *Don Victoriano Salado Álvarez y la Conversación en México*. Editorial Cultura. Mexico City, 1932.

Vigil, José María. *Reseña Incompleta de la Literatura Mexicana*. (Courtesy of the National Library of Mexico.)

Wilde, Oscar. *Intentions*. Leipzig, Bernard Tauchnitz.

PRELIMINARY NOTES ON THE THEATER

I

THE THEATER is a perfidious profession which should have a feminine appellation. The dramatist needs to have his head both in the clouds and on the ground. Is it a question of the sublime dialogue of a dynamic character, of the deceived husband, of the artist in apotheosis, of the victorious warrior, of the tired and triumphant lover? Let us pause for a moment: the doorway is low and narrow for all, the stellar character, husband, artist, warrior or lover, whether the entrance should be from the left or the right. Let us be more specific.

The theater is a delightful craft, and it should have a feminine designation. It is animated sculpture and, like any artistic creation, it goes beyond the conventionalisms of art and is limited only by the conventionalism of the artist. In the theater rhetoric is not the salvation of a drama anymore than marble is the salvation of a piece of sculpture.

Furthermore, only a great tailor is comparable to a great dramatist. Harmony of color, differences of cut, an appreciation for the season of the year and the time of the day, graceful pleats and the total elimination of wrinkles, a profound knowledge of the results of the various postures, all of these elements should exist in both clothing and characters. It is well known that, in spite of the tailors, clothes are unbecoming or completely unattractive in direct proportion to the educational defects of those who wear them, people who only seem attractive when seated and who spoil their suit as soon as they stand up. The actor at times mistreats terribly the character he is interpreting, for example, when he sits down. I have seen actors who give the impression of sitting down on their character. This should lead the dramatist who possesses an awareness of, and love for, his work to an apprenticeship of patience, and from there to a control of his craft and to a triumphant tyranny without having to devote a large part of his life to the analysis of each one of his actors. In the same way, the tailor — to end this parallel in an acute angle — finishes by imposing his will and dressing his ungainly client. This is true, and this is all I have to say, because he does not need to know each one of his parishioners — which would be a mark of unacceptable submission in an artist —, but must know the various parts of his handiwork: cloth, cut, interlinings, linings, buttons and buttonholes, and not make use of the materials which are indispensable for a jacket in making a pair of trousers.

The dramatist of today frequently suffers from cinematographic flashes and, even worse, literary hallucinations. It is a confusion which is the product of this tower of Babel which is the motion picture with its avant garde in Joinville, its songs in English, its dialogues in shameful Spanish or in peddler's French. I believe, nevertheless, to the honor of the body, that the boundaries between the theater and the motion picture are still known and perceptible, and that if they are violated it is only intentionally, as occurs in international politics. I think, furthermore, that there is throughout the world a group of men who aspire to unify and universalize a new theatrical language. It would be terrible for me personally if this were not so, for I would have to continue writing theatrical works no matter what. The theater seems to me to be that proverbial fountain to which the French refer when they say "Whoever has drunk will drink more," or that weaving of the one hundred baskets of our own proverb. They have an entrance, but the exit is still unknown.

I should like, before going further — if I can go further — to state what I believe to be the most distinctive and visible boundary between the theater and the motion picture. In order not to stumble in taking this step, I gladly accept the words of that gentleman who maintains that the motion picture, particularly that of the present time, will degenerate into a museum of present-day life: collections of clothes, of gestures of voices, of world events, of regional dances and, finally, of customs which will, in a century, be worthy of only a glass case and a classification. And what is a museum? I confess that each time I enter one it would be difficult for me to resist the temptation to open my umbrella, if I used an umbrella. The fog and mist of antiquity, a museum is a course in physical history and nothing more. The motion picture, consequently, has already found its true reason for existing. We hope that it fulfills it, because among the most difficult things in this world there is one thing which is very difficult, and that is to find our own path. And there is a yet more difficult thing: to follow it. History has, moreover, grave defects. Friederich Nietzsche, whom I shall invite to take a seat in this article if you will permit me, opines that "by dint of investigating one's origins one is transformed into a crab. The historian sees backward; he finishes by BELIEVING backward." And, in my opinion, one of the most serious defects of history is, therefore, the historian.

Then let us leave the pride of being history to the motion picture. If the theater is modest, it will be satisfied with the immense field of fiction. The motion picture will be history; but the theater will be — I think — what it has always pretended to be: the tale. The historian is only, in the end, a serious tale-teller and, therefore, a frustrated one, for the inner life of men is found in complete form in the tale. Let us take Napoleon signing the treaty of Tilsit, and we will feel obliged to turn our backs on him, respectfully if we must, but turn them on him nevertheless. On the other hand, let us observe Napoleon directing the performances at Talma, and we shall enjoy him extraordinarily. Let us see Henry Ford in the motion picture museum reinforcing the principle of the comfort of trans- portation — if that can be said — among the upper social classes and inaugurating the factory-nation; this may be admired, but coldly. Let us imagine him — if we believe sibylline voices — in the depths of his life as a man who does not know how to read or write, and we shall feel all his strength with astonishment, with interest and even with love, for that which we love most is not what is revealed to us, but what we discover. In the anecdote are the instinct and the originality of the human being. Man is made of three materials: one of atavism, another of education and another absolutely autoctonous one, which has its origin within him and which dies with him. Notice how the autoctonous material within the anecdote emerges from the human being. The anecdote, then, is the cause or the development of a situation.

What is the theater but a study of a situation and of a certain number of individuals put to the test in that situation? In the dramatic work, as in the private life of an individual, causative factors converge which are freely labelled meteorological phenomena or fate; hunger, ambition, crime or social needs; indifference and strength, or immorality and religion. The man who leaves his home bound for his office, and arrives there on time and conscientiously fulfills his task and returns home with no problem and has dinner without a disagreement with his wife, is living his history. If his work is noble and his example elegant, he will go on with time to become an element of universal history. But the same man, subjected to the vagaries of a shower and obliged to take refuge under a doorway and to spend an hour watching those who, like himself, are seeking shelter against the storm and are running into each other and jostling one another, or thrust by the same fate into a conversation and from there into an adventure in that incidental hour of his life, is an element for the anecdote, and the angle for a theatrical situation. I fear that the example may be too coarse, but I hope to establish the highly anecdotal significance of the theater. Having finished this, let us return to the dramatist.

It has never been more difficult to write than at the present time, because it has never been easier nor has as much been written as now. It is almost a matter of self-esteem not to write because, from a great industrialist to a manufacturer of cookies, passing through generals, sopranos, boxers, movie stars, swindlers, airplane stowaways, prison guards, fashion experts and perfume dealers, everyone feels obliged to put in a book what the Americans odiously call "one's experiences." The theater, fortunately, has been preserved without stagnating within a particular area which has the marvelous quality of being uniquely difficult. Outside of one essential difficulty, which consists of the meaning of the theater, it offers several pitfalls. Technicalities, for example, constitute one, even though they may be limited to a question of quotations and nomenclature. What was called from Shakespeare to Alfred de Musset — with great propriety — a stage, is now called a frame, etcétera. The tragedy has degenerated into a play, and the latter employs the two masks of Thalia; the "high" drama is only a drama, and the drama is only an astrakhan. A greater difficulty, doubtlessly, is the question of scenic matters. The hurried Shakespeare was satisfied with a piece of open land for the most heart-rending scene about King Lear, who was dispossessed, persecuted and old.

We are a little intimated by the set since is has ceased to be art in order to become comfort — the only goddess —, even when it attempts to be artistic comfort. We need a thousand small things, but I trust that this great need will pass from us, at least in the theater. Mr. O'Neill has already rejected it; but let us confess that he has achieved it by going with arms and baggage over to the farthest extreme of discomfort: to wit the poor *Emperor Jones*. In short, technicalities only present difficulties as long as they are not unique to each dramatist.

The third pitfall: there is a point upon which the vitality of any theatrical work depends: language. No one needs to be more grammatical than the dramatist, whether he adjusts himself to previously established norms or whether he subjects the grammer of his language to his own power. This is more than a pitfall. It is, in a modern simile, a terrible vacuum cleaner. May the gods preserve us from the presence of the worn out madrigal on the stage. But may they also equally preserve us from the unbearable visitation of the slang expression and its numerous framily. G. Bernard Shaw weaves into the prologue to *The Dark Lady of the Sonnets* an ingenious crown of praise to Shakespeare, himself a collector of popular sayings. And I classify the praise as ingenious because at the end Shaw says: "Shakespeare did admirably. I am doing the same." It is true of both. With regard to Shakespeare, I consider it useless to say that he had the necessary mental wherewithal for, keeping intact the essence of popular sayings, ennobling the latter in the assembly of lofty thoughts, of sentiments, and of exceptional anecdotes which presides over his tragedies. He knew how to use the colloquial expression just as a distinguished man knows how to shoot dice or billiards. But keep in mind that he is, above all else, a man who injects life into his language, and to vivify means not just to give life to, but also to furnish the means for living it logically. Mr. Shaw, for his part, has seen himself betrayed in the most historic manner in many instances by his translators. He is much less profane than he seems in the editions published by Aguilar, and ten times more ingenious, although his socialism may not permit him to create types destined to feed the sacred fire of the heroes, except perhaps in *Pygmalion*. However, this genius of prologues writes principally in English. Once again, insofar as language is concerned, I permit myself to insist that the dramatic work — a creation and not a reproduction — cannot be enclosed in any other conventionalisms than those of the artist, its author.

There is an additional danger for dramatists: they are leaders of multitudes in a direct way. The multitudes do not need for someone to lead them toward what they desire, but toward what they do not have and should have. The novelist, the poet and the philosopher lead only selected multitudes in which each unity has a value as a unity. The dramatist sees himself obliged to lead unprepared and unselected multitudes over which he must reign as the great unity. From this indispensible tyranny to a fall is a short distance if one does not preserve an unalterable prestige of superiority, for there are playwrights who believe themselves obligated to be more common than the public they pretend to educate.

I realize that someone might wish to interrupt me in order to ask: "And what about reality? Is a member of the agrarian community of Mexico going to speak the same as an educated person from the Teatro Ulises?" I take advantage of the pause to quote from Oscar Wilde: "It is the spectator and not life which art really reflects." Let us reflect the spectator, then, but artistically: with a little exaggeration, with convexity or with concavity. Let us make him recognize himself in a more noble reflection which may lead him to a desire for his own ennoblement. The father who instead of teaching his children to speak traditionally learns to babble like them, will see himself shunned by them when they reach the age of reason even though they may applaud him at the beginning.

Another head is shaking. Over there I see a finger being raised. The question is: "And all of this is true of the Mexican theater?"

Indeed, my dear sir — I answer —. I did not wish to refer to any other, The Mexican theater is, simply, the theater.

(*El Universal Ilustrado*. Mexico City, D. F. September 10, 1931. No. 748, volume XV.)

II

The writer of today is a civilized writer, so civilized at times that he ceases to be a writer. Perhaps the strength which elevates him to a height equal to that achieved by the primitive writer is rooted in this point, in spite of its inconsistency. He is a compiler of past epochs and an adapter. He lacks a panoramic imagination, but he has acquired a sharp sense for small details and their large importance. He is, in short, a hybrid of psychology and culture. He imposes himself on the multitudes because of his knowledge and his faculties of selection just as the primitive imposed himself through his imagination and his strength. He brings with his aftermath of consequences the broadening of a universal need for culture in the diverse social and artistic entities to the extent that the positively ignorant man will soon be a magnificent product of contrast, rare and almost precious. Fortunately, there is a limit to the civilization of the modern world: each person receives a serving of culture proportionate to the dish he can manage, a dish which, as irreverently as incidentally, represents here the intelligence.

Fleeing from the current of the social classes, I wish to indicate that one of the benefits of this system consists of the unavoidable civilization of the actor and, of course, of the masses who attend the theater. In the first case the effect was immediate: the uncultured and temperamental actor has been removed from the payroll and dismissed from the stage. In the second case the outcome is slower because the actor has only the theater, while the public has the theater among, and after, many other things. The public will be civilized by virtue of the actor's degree of civilization, and I understand, furthermore, that in other countries both catechisms have been completely achieved. The point of departure is simple. The world reweighs and reassesses its values daily; by making a study of the professional runner it conceived of the airplane, and by cataloguing the distinctive and (I cannot resist the temptation to say it) qualitative defects of the classic butler it is inventing the discreet and odious automat of popular acceptance.

In order to write modern theater, authors have had to collect believable and unbelievable situation, to traffic with the Greek tragedians and the Latin playwrights; to be introduced to the mystery plays, farces and miracle plays of the Middle Ages; to sit down at the sumptuous and magnanimous table of the Golden Age; to attend the solemn banquets of Shakespeare, the breakfast of Molière and the unequalled wakes of Calderón. After all of this, being acquainted in detail with their age and living the poor but inexchangeable private life of the theater as well, they have gone so far as to write *Six Characters in Search of an Author* when, for example, they call themselves Luigi Pirandello.

A similar program of mountainous and difficult topography becomes fatal for the student of scenic arts. I suppose that this is the reason why the students at the conservatories of other countries prepare their final examinations on the basis of an average *Hamlet,* of *The Bandits* of Schiller, or of some fables of Jean de la Fontaine, which are not original but are at least classical, or of the romance which says:

> Since I, out of justice
> availed myself of your respect...

This explains why, like true athletes, those students may pass from this item to the risky game of Messrs. Bernard Shaw, Pirandello, O'Neill, Rice, Hecht, Gogol, etc.

I hasten to point out that in other countries — Russia, for example and France — the theater constitutes a national institutional custom, comparable to the bullfights or the fascinating cockfights of our land. Hence the reason, following the trail of actors crowned with the green laurel, the name in capital letters and the golden salary, why so many young people rush to the conservatories which dispense such an education. There is a traditional compromise drawn up between faithful audiences, good writers, good actors and good students from good conservatories. The fact that declamation is less important in those countries than good diction in general, and than grammar, facilitates all this. Grammar, with a sprinkling of etymology where possible, is indispensable for avoiding that the actors put a dramatic emphasis on words with a misleading connotation and poor meaning, stratiform-like, or no emphasis on words of modest scope and good stock. Diction and grammar, in short, are necessary because one of the greatest enemies of the voice is declamation, and the voice — I regret having to say it — is the only tangible fortune of the actor. An unpleasant face, insufficient height, these can be corrected with make-up and devices, and can be hidden with a little imagination. The voice, to put it thus, is exhibited in the nude. Depending upon whether it is disagreeable or uneducated it irritates us, it offends us, it inclines us toward evil. If we were magistrates, we would condemn those who spoke to us with that kind of a voice, and I have no idea how many judges have probably decreed such a sentence in times of digestive travail, but I pay them my tribute here.

Although it is true that we do not speak an impeccable Spanish in Mexico, and that we have lost the notion of aesthetics regarding the voice which consists of phonetic values, we do have a language with a pleasant sound which the slightest carelessness transforms into a vulgar and intemperate scandal which is bothersome in everyday situations in life and is intolerable in the theater. The human voice has emancipated itself from the discipline of music not just because it is the most precious instrument of sound. Spanish, which is not a language of hues but of colors, is capable of reaching the most marvelous melodiousness in a well educated voice subjected to precise and regulated control and color. A scholar with his voice and brain trained to declaim and understand, for example, *Life is a Dream,* could in my opinion be a good professional actor in *Grand Hotel* or in *Dynamo.* I trust that we will be offered such a spectacle in a future conservatory in Mexico some day.

After the voice, what can be said of the gesture? The anchor of renovation employed by the actors in *Proteus,* by Francisco Monterde, was terribly heavy and made several of them founder. It is an anchor which at times weighs more than the boat, and it is called naturalness.

The theater is not natural. If it were, I would not go to the theater. Modern works are not, fortunately, natural. Imagination is not natural. It is even less natural than that of the magnificent monster called the *Orestiade,* by our civilized writer. Shall I be forced, furthermore, to say that art is not natural? Imagination today is twisted, is narrow, deforms its opulent Attic shape, adorns itself with exquisite toiletries, changes the fashions of its four seasons, complicates itself to the point of simplicity.

The naturalness of an actor cannot be the same as that of the audience which is watching him. If it were, the actor should simply buy himself some opera glasses and seat himself in the auditorium.

The naturalness of the actor consists in being natural in harmony with the epoch, the atmosphere, the words of the work which he is interpreting. The author has manufactured a new country for him and, in order to have the right to inhabit it, it is necessary for the actor to immerse himself in that country, for him to copy its colors in dawns and sunsets, for him to limit himself to its horizons, for him to be BORN in that country, and for him to live and die in it with the strength of an ancient man. Otherwise, he is only an undesirable alien.

The spectator is only a guest who is going to contemplate in the theater a limitless life of which his own is a simple reflection which aspires to be greater and better. Nations alone, through politics, disguise themselves with the well known mask in order to present to the illustrious outsider a caricature of the country which it represents. The theater is more than a country.

The theater is marvelously false. It is a more or less large and dusty platform which accepts all sets, which projects all tendencies, which collects all passions. In fairness I shall say, in order to give a more precise idea, that the world is almost as large as the theater.

(*El Universal Ilustrado*. September 24, 1931. No. 750, volume XV.)

III

It is maintained that the modern theater is using motion picture techniques like agricultural fertilizer, and — in order to be discreet — works like *Mélo,* by Henri Bernstein, in which the close-up, the greatest triumph of the cinematographer, is used with long-shot results.

I pick up, by chance, a volume of classical theater and examine it. It contains *Anthony and Cleopatra.* First act, first scene: a room in the palace of Cleopatra, in Alexandria; second scene: another room in the same palace; third scene: another room in the same palace; fourth scene: a room in the house of Caesar, in Rome, etc. If this is not a motion picture scenario, nothing else is. Then I recall the early movies which were so dreadful and theatrical generally and which had such panoramic clever escapades and natural outdoor settings, weapons which still inspired terror in directors. Little by little the latter gain more confidence, cultivate, irrigate and make flourish an entire garden of cinematographic resources. But they have a mortal enemy: silence. Among the different formulas suggested by historical precedent for conquering an enemy there is the humiliating and perfidious method of changing him into — a friend. Mimicry, a minor art form of classical extraction, is gradually revived, and eliminates step by step the need for the voice, in which the most perfect form of expression had resided up to that time, and announces symptoms of apotheosis — a dangerous illness — in the works of Charles Spencer Chaplin. In artistic matters anything which subsists on its own resources and makes us believe that it has no others is art. All else is merely formulas for creating art or second hand criticism. Hence the motion picture is transformed into an art form and is freed from the requirements of the theater.

A digression imposes itself and transports me back to the first encounter between the motion picture and the theater. The stage directors of the sixteenth and seventeenth centuries must have been admirable as producers of the cinematographic theater of their times. The robust and fertile imagination of the tragedians and playwrights imposed laborious tasks upon them, and although it is true that they frequently resorted to hai-kai descriptions of the imaginary settings, making use of the poster of felicitious recollection, this in no way diminishes the quality of their variegated and sincere efforts. Likewise, the fact that the imagination of the audience might be applied to a supplicatory vision of the stage presentation in no way succeeded in corrupting the magnificent imaginative independence of the dramatists. Civilization later accumulated the restrictions in the theater and its academy, and it was in this way, after the first misstep, that we reached the odious French plays of the *fin-de-siècle,* with repercussions up to the beginnings of the post-war period in which the congregation, as if by law and under the sanction of persons in places of no interest or beauty, has offered us the most absurd examples of ineptness and narrowness. There are plays of that sort in which it appears as if all the characters might have been employed by the inspiration of the authors only to reach, panting in the last act, places distant from their homes. I omit Maurice Donnay from this odious generality.

In spite of everything, however, the theater has always preserved in its structure a reason for existing with the functions of a heart:

it studies or imagines the tragedy of man, naked within four walls.
Four walls inside of which to love, to be born, to murder, to
dream, to die, for everything which we cannot do decently in the
middle of the street in any part of the world.

I return to the motion picture, which has no personal resources
or private wellsprings and which has consequently lighted the fuse
of restlessness in the theater. It is at this time that the dramatist
turns toward that apochryphal Klondike in search of the golden
demon of novelty, determined to capture his soul. But the motion
picture cannot become stagnant, it is continually studied, subjected
to exercises which must develop it, is has even conquered sound
and the voice and, the Napoleon of art, it revives and repeats the
verses of Mr. Hugo: "The future is mine!" Let us answer with
the same music:

> No, the future belongs to no one,
> Sir! the future belongs to God!

Now it needs (should one say alas?) to submit itself to its own
conquest. Greatness is like that. In order to take advantage of the
voice it must, after the operetta and the night club act, shut itself
away within four walls where, following the vagaries of dialogue,
the passions, interests and ideas of the characters may be unleased.
It is true that it covers those four walls with photographic discov-
eries, and that it preserves the crown of the close-up; but it has
created theatrical necessities for itself, and it has contracted a new
mésalliance with no visible possibilities for divorce.

Who, in short, is imitating whom?

I have spoken already of the anecdotal significance of the
theater, and I now will attempt to describe the essentially allegorical
significance of its technique, a significance which it is necessary
to revive in order to separate the theater from the motion picture
definitively.

Have you read, sir, *The Inspector,* a play by Nicholas Vasi-
lievich Gogol? In the event that the answer is affirmative, recall
the fourth act: "Room in the Mayor's house." Thumbing through
a history of the Russian theater composed by R. Fülop-Miller and
J. Gregor, I found, among a thousand other admirable things,
which border on geniality even when they do not completely pos-

Teatro Mayerhold. "El Inspector". Esscena del soborno.

XXVI.   Teatro Mayerhold.   *The Inspector.*   Bribe   Scene

sess it, the photograph with which I will complete this article and which seems to me to be a conclusive document with regard not only to the theatrical talent of the Russians but especially with regard to the allegorical significance of the theater. Around the false Inspector, you will recall, there has unfolded a heterogeneous group of interested parties: all the officials are attempting to bribe him: his servant, out of devotion, watches over him, and the wife and daughter of the Mayor have found in him all the temptations of the city and the court. The set of the Teatro Mayerhold reflects the same spirit of the situation, the concern which each character has for himself and the mistrust which motivates the others. Each official awaits his turn in order to play his role in the bribe; but, HOW does each one wait? In what particular frame of mind? This is what the photograph shows us. Each one fears destitution, prison or Siberian exile. But it is necessary for the audience to understand it, words are not always sufficient, and in this way the audience is brought into the situation and experiences it intensely, as if it were its own. In order to achieve this effect, which is a part of the larger scene according to the analytical system, nothing more than the admirable interpretive sense of the stage director is required in order to surprise and satisfy the audience, for the effect has not been obtained by thinking of the latter but of the work to be interpreted.

It may be said by way of contradiction that there are no real rooms with that number of doors, and this is true, but shame on him who says such a thing. Who formulated the rule by which the theater is obligated to follow the same line as circumstantial reality, and what is that rule? I do not understand why the creative work of the author must contain a flaw because of the reproduction of the stage director, nor can I conceive of photographic necessities within the theater. The same emphasis, the same sublimation which the voice of the actors requires, is a vital element in scenic technique. Every attempt at art carries within its principles that of becoming unforgettable. The only advantage of common things lies in the fact that they are the exclusive domain of forgetfulness.

Just as the autonomous art *par excellence* is music, the theater is the most eclectic one known. It has ties with music, painting, sculpture, poetry and fashion, and it has mastered the most noble instruments that exist like a great performer. Hence its seductive force, its binding power, its prodigious vitality in spite of the condition of an ephemeral phenomenon which the voice, the only real means of life it possesses, imposes upon it.

The theater has all these things for allegorizing life, but I take the liberty of informing stage directors that it loses all of that when it is pushed by any enthusiasm to the extreme of allegorizing the allegory.

(*El Universal Ilustrado,* October 1, 1931. No. 751, volume XV.)

IV

A gentleman known by the name of René Magnon de Montaigu, a cousin of Fontenelle and allegedly a disciple of Jean Baptiste Poquelin, was responsible for the establishment of the Danish theater in the national language two hundred years ago, abolishing the drama in French which had been rooted in Denmark up until that time. As a curious aside it is necessary to recall that the stage director Montaigu knew no Danish, and had to have the plays explained to him before he undertook to direct their production.

Our equivalent of Montaigu, the gentleman who made the worthwhile suggestion that we not pronounce the *c* and the *z* and the *ll* on our stages in the Castilian fashion, is today as forgotten as Montaigu. Furthermore, he gave us a very meager independence. It is almost a shame that we do not have, together with the liberator, a language with the characteristics of Danish. A language which is not a subsidiary of another possesses a perfection and a racial strength. Mexico would be saved, theatrically speaking, if we were all Indians or Spaniards. We have, without being able to take advantage of them properly, all the elements of the high tragedy: all the poisons which struggle among themselves, an ideal for revolution, an ideal for peace and a healthy opposition against those and other ideals; our drama has been the oldest in America and, nevertheless, it is one of the least interesting because we are lacking something. We lack the hallmark.

Among all the art forms which serve to identify a race the theater is most assuredly, the most conclusive. One would have to find a miraculous formula in order to confuse a French play with a Russian one, or an English drama with an Italian one. The compact flower of a particular race, the theater is the true hallmark of nations.

Because of the frequent absence of a neighbor seated in the chair next to mine, I have had to ask myself a model question one hundred times while witnessing Aztec dances, at the Tenayuca pyramid, or the folklore theater, of the Europeanizing or Europeanized artistic manifestations from the dress circle or the gallery. Is this Mexico? And it has been the same in the street. The question has come back with the persistence of an installment radio salesman because of contemplating fashionable old hats, nudism, English, Maya and Oaxaca restaurants, curio shops, and every migratory thing which has come to settle in such a noble and hospitable land.

Previously, after taking a bath of Spanish astrakhan in what is termed in journalistic jargon "the Coliseum of Dolores," or following an excellent *Topaze* at the Arbeu, I frequently engaged in the impertinence of asking myself about the Mexican theater. Over a period of several years I have been able to discover what we are lacking, to observe the stepping stones and the gardens which interbreeding has left in this enormous jewel which is Mexico, and to sense the ethnic transcendancy of the moment. All of us today are at one extreme or the other. Importers, contrabandists at times, of fashions and fancies here; preservers, guardians or exploiters of birds of a Neolithic past, however sublime, but a past, there. There is still nothing in the middle. I have understood that those of us on one extreme and the other are often selfish, always protecting our particular private interests and reluctantly working a minimum day in order to fill what is empty, to build bridges over the ravine, to fertilize our broad expanse of sterile land, and for other similar reasons. I know that persons in whose field I find myself are making individual efforts for the development of a Mexican theater. But nothing else, apart from that, is happening. The others are empresarios who consider themselves sublime psychologists when they give utterance to platitudes and conjugate the verb "Give-the-public-what-it-wants," or the verb "Feed-on-the-stupid-public," or the verb "Beware-of-Mexican-authors." The others are illiterate translators who command hypothetical foreign tongues and who modify and correct at their leisure the works which they are betraying. The others are a disoriented public which has tired of all of this and out of boredom has entered a motion picture theater.

A modest sweep over the panoramas of the European theater is sufficient to perceive the area of the national importance of the theater with regard to artistic values, educational material and even political propaganda. Everywhere the theater has begun as an aspiration in the hands of interested members of a social middle class, as a need perceived by young or old intellectuals, and it has been everywhere a tribunal for criticism and an institution of learning. Just as in France with Molière and Beaumarchais, and in Russia with Gogol, Griboiedov and Chekov, or in England with Bernard Shaw, it has been the forerunner of the great political, social and intellectual transformations. The recent and visible fact that the theater in the United States has once again taken on a national importance which it did not possess a few years ago should be enough to put us on the alert. It is true, however, that there are some means of communications which have not yet been improved by busy Science. A certain Mr. Baeza, a Spanish translator of some foreign books who says he translates textually, "All children have wings" or, in a closer version, "We are all children of God," for "All God's Chillun Got Wings," and I shall say no more, states in an introductory note to his translations of the theater of Eugene O'Neill that, in his judgement, the path to the literary theater in the United States is a consequence of the motion picture. I will not quote the long paragraph in which this claim is made, and I prefer not to say that there has never been literature in the motion picture, that literature is a higher course, a terminal degree in the world, and that literature has no opportunity of any sort worthy of it in an industry like that of the motion picture. It is no less correct, therefore, that the theater is developing intensely in the United States. It is only that this development, understandable to the common man as a result of the fatigue of watching motion pictures, is ultimately, the result of an ethnic phenomenon. The United States of America — it has no more distinctive name — has begun to constitute a race at present following upon the tumultuous immigrations and multiple transfusions from the oldest Occidental bloodlines. Among its latest requirements as a race which is approaching the age of maturity are, particularly, that of the theater, that of the intellectual and literary spirit and of a national intellect. All that was great which the United States possessed previously in this regard was not American but was the intention to create something which would become American.

The same Mr. Baeza, who is a better compiler of statistical data than translator, shows clearly that the development of the theater in the United States took on a purely municipal character. All the cities provided facilities for the establishment in each locality of amateur theaters, of auditoriums intended for theatrical spectacles of all intellectual lineages; the universities needed dramatic groups and Harvard, Princeton and Yale created "true conservatories where such competent authorities as Professors Baker and Stuart have trained a nucleus of writers and actors who, like Eugene O'Neill (who studied with Baker), were not long in becoming famous." (R. Baeza. *Op. cit.*)

Of course, this work in the United States is similar to, or rather derived from, that carried out in Russia, especially if one starts with the establishment of the bourgeois theater in the same way that what happened with the essentially modern theater of Russia constitutes a phenomenon which was observed previously in the literary countries of Western Europe. We would not imitate the United States, then, if we were to try to intensify the love for, and the life of, the theater in Mexico. That would only constitute an act of submission to an ethnic law and the fulfillment of involuntary functions like the growth and change of sets of teeth.

We need one hundred theaters like the one which the Department of Fine Arts has just created, one hundred amateur groups and a Conservatory where the dramatic art may be taught. Resolved: we need to bleed the national budget innocently so that competent persons may go to study theatrical systems abroad. Resolved: we need to do the same in actual practice as many times as may be necessary.

I must go now; but, if you wish, we may meet again next Thursday at the same time and in the same place.

(*El Universal Ilustrado,* October 22, 1931. No. 754, volume XV.)

V

I seem to have forgotten something. What was it? After assuring myself that I have cigarettes with me, a handkerchief, a tie and, in general, all that one requires in order to go out into the street without risking the danger of being termed a pioneer — as Villaurrutia says — of nudism, I return to my home. It was not an appointment; I have the anti-social habit of never forgetting them or, to make a more pleasant exception, almost never forgetting them. What was it? Let us examine this voluminous file which says "Notes on the Theater." Not without impatience, I lay aside "Polemics," "Arguments," "Dictation," "Subversive Discussion," "Inevitable Outcries," "Expressive Silences"... Ah! I recognize a word by the last syllable: SPECIALIZATION. This is it. I open it suspiciously because I am accustomed now to find the wrappings of many words empty, and those of others filled with unmarketable gibberish, like the "sundries section" where we all as children bought our pencils, notebooks and portable inkwells for school, or the caramel bonbons and clay puppets for the pleasures of outdoor use at that age.

Specialization. It is full; it will be necessary to empty it little by little. Shakespeare appears first. Shakespeare again? Why? I recall. Literature and Baconianism aside, it is now a matter of William Shakespeare, specialist in the theater. Of twenty volumes which constitute the edition of his works with which I am most familiar, nineteen contain comedies and tragedies, and only the twentieth contains the matrimonial sonnets dedicated to Mr. W. H., the cruel ones inflicted upon the Dark Lady, "The Passionate Pilgrim," etc. This lyric work is nothing more than the featherwork on the marvelous literary costume of Shakespeare. The rest is drama. And not just that which was written for posterity nor that which was created out of necessity for the public at that time. In the same way, and more specifically, is life made of a single sound, of a single color; the same is true of a life in the theater, whether it is spent writing plays or directing performances, or dreaming of laying the first stone in a national theater. In Shakespeare what dazzles is, with the indulgence of the antipathetic Mr. Stendhal, what I shall term the theater-passion.

Now Lope de Rueda appears. Both author and actor, he carries, according to Cervantes, all his paraphernalia in a miserable sack, "and his theater consisted of four or five benches in a square and four to six platforms upon them which were about four hands above the ground; the set was an old blanket stretched between two ropes from one side to the other, which formed what they called a dressing room, behind which the musicians were performing without a guitar..." Why quote more? Such were the miracles of that time.

Among other Lopes appears the one named Vega, who wrote over one thousand plays or, for greater accuracy, wrote plays throughout his life. That century whose quorum consists of the writers already mentioned, of Juan Ruiz de Alarcón, of Pedro Calderón de la Barca, and of Molière himself, was the century of the great specialists. But it is Molière, particularly, who perfects specialization in the theater to the extreme of exhibiting his agony on the stage, and who offers, because of his borrowings from Alarcón, the most perfect example of the modern specialist, followed since that time up to Sacha Guitry and Tristan Bernard by the admirable practicality of the French theater. I extract yet another name from the lengthy word: O'Neill, who has only written drama and for whom the four unities would be uninteresting if they were not the material of which plays are made.

It would be superfluous to erect the wall of names which could be constructed, but without it, to be honest, it may be understood that it is impossible to devote less than a lifetime to the theater. Even when one does it is necessary to ask that one be excused by it, to turn one's pockets inside out and say: "I am sorry, but I do not have any more."

All art is the fruit of specialization, but the latter seems to me to be more necessary in the theater than elsewhere. Any art form presupposes a more or less arduous struggle, but always a ceaseless one. However, with the exception of the theater, it is always a struggle between the artist and the raw materials. In the theater the conflict develops between the artist and his work. The only creation which is not finished in the dialogue with its creator is a play. The poet, the sculptor, the painter and the musician all live in harmonious union with their works, guiding themselves by means of the rule of thumb of the perfect housewife, everything in proportion. The playwright has to separate himself from his work and wait for it to come back to him, something which it frequently fails to do. What is worse he exposes himself to the possibility, also frequent, that the faithless one may not return alone. Specialization in the theater, then, seems to me to be indispensable even if only for the purpose of studying the pathology of its infidelity.

Strewn on the bottom of "Specialization" I find several letters, in a pattern which is as logical as any other, which spell the work "Lack." What does this mean? In Mexico we are lacking specialization. Outside of Eslava, about whom nothing is known beyond the *Colloquies,* outside of Ruiz de Alarcón, of Gorostiza, of Fernando Calderón and of Peón y Contreras, the only ones classifiable as specialists until the nineteenth century, the remaining dramatists in Mexico, leaving an indulgent silence over the recurring unknowns, are nothing more than tourists, at times distinguished tourists, but who, if they are interesting upon their arrival, are disillusioning when they board the train to return to the country of their origin. Sor Juana, torn as she is between lyric poetry and the theater but who is in my opinion more lofty and complete in the former than in the latter, cannot be subjected to classification. I have noticed that in all periods persons who are the owners of more or less extensive literary plantations have sown a comedy, a drama, a tragedy or, like the indescribable Mr. Juan A. Mateos, an adaptation of some French *feuilleton* in them. And what is more serious, I have also noticed that after this our abject poverty in matters concerning the theater has permitted them to be considered dramatists. The specialists which I have mentioned offer a robust production worthy of profound study and adaptable to specialized courses. But after them there is something lacking which relates them to each other and which combines their legacy. There is a lack of theatrical literature which should be found between Juan Ruiz de Alarcón and Juan A. Mateos, let us call it a literary middle class which is compact and harmonious from which can emerge our next genius of letters as the great animators of national life have emerged from the social middle class from France to Russia, and from there downward.

In general, we have literates and we lack literature.

I do not mean to imply that no theatrical works have been written in Mexico. On the contrary, a great deal has been written; if not, let Francisco Monterde, who has found so many works and who, fortunately, has failed to find many others in his patient search, deny it. But nothing was suitable, neither the efforts of a Romantic delayed by the poor communications of the defunct nineteenth century — why mention the two previous ones? — nor the one which attempted to describe customs, nor the one which was ceaselessly exploited in the parody of the adaptation which extends from the missionaries of the Conquest to the popular actors of today. Why? Our customs are no worse than those of other countries; they are as much customs as their counterparts. To describe them in the theater, two things were lacking: technique and point of view. The one which was used — making once again exceptions of the previous exceptions — was too low. It was, to be precise, the one which the first of the Wilhelms of Germany exiled in Dorn, or rather Wilhelm the Second, calls the point of view of the frog. This is the reason why we do not have a theater of customs, because the authors observed them from the bottom upward instead of doing the reverse like the poets, on the other hand, who have been exceptional in our land. And poetry alone does not imply a summit. In art everything is loftiness. I hope that this will change now that our youth is putting on the last existing crown: the crown of airs.

Furthermore, a healthy immigration is taking place slowly but surely in the lands of the theater. Let everyone deal with the theme which he prefers or describe the doctrine which enslaves him, it will all be theater.

It is true that the authors are suffering from the disease of a dearth of trained actors, but a remedy may exist for this as well. In 1875, President Lerdo de Tejada supported a conservatory whose failure was due, in general, to works by Mexican authors. Now that authors have a more refined, independent and complete physiognomy, that support is most lacking.

The Russians utilized the theater, let it be recalled, as a system for propaganda for the ideas of social transformation, just as the Spanish missionaries utilized it following the practice of the Middle Ages for the purpose of evangelization. In both instances the learning imparted to the people was rapid. And it is curious to note, reviewing the history of Mexico, that if in 1810 we had had a half dozen great Mexican actors the war of Independence would not have lasted for more than two years.

RODOLFO USIGLI

(*El Universal Ilustrado,* November 5, 1931. No. 756, volume XV.)

INDEX OF ILLUSTRATIONS

Engravings by Tostado.
*Reproductions of Codices
by* Enrique Corona G.

ALPHABETICAL INDEX